FREDERIC WILLIAM MAITLAND

"In an age of great historians I think that Maitland was the greatest."
SIR WILLIAM HOLDSWORTH

"Maitland is one of the immortals."
SIR MAURICE POWICKE

UNIVERSITY OF CALIFORNIA PRESS
BERKELEY AND LOS ANGELES-1960

FREDERIC WILLIAM
MAITLAND
HISTORIAN

selections from his writings
edited, with an introduction
by ROBERT LIVINGSTON SCHUYLER

UNIVERSITY OF CALIFORNIA PRESS
BERKELEY AND LOS ANGELES, CALIFORNIA
CAMBRIDGE UNIVERSITY PRESS
LONDON, ENGLAND

LIBRARY OF CONGRESS CATALOG CARD NUMBER: 60-9650
DESIGNED BY HARRY MARKS

Preface

A word should be said about the general editorial principles followed in compiling this collection of writings by Frederic William Maitland. Because the book is intended for students of history and of historical method rather than for the Maitland specialist, the original footnotes, with two or three exceptions, have been omitted. In choosing and editing the selections themselves, I have tried to follow a policy of rigid selectivity, restricting myself to those passages that seem best to illustrate what needs to be said of Maitland as a historian. This has meant that severe excisions had occasionally to be made—sometimes only a sentence or two, sometimes a couple of paragraphs, sometimes ten or a dozen pages in one fell swoop—if the book were to be kept within reasonable compass. In order to prevent the pages from being riddled with the resulting ellipses, these have not been indicated except where they occur at the beginning or in the middle of paragraphs. A reader who wishes to turn to the originals should for the most part have no difficulty in readily spotting what has been dropped and what has been retained.

Except for changing single quotation marks to double, no attempt has been made to standardize or to make uniform the variety of styles of punctuation or spelling of the originals. It is hoped that readers accustomed to shifting from British to American sources will not find this unduly disturbing.

In preparing the introduction to these selections, I have drawn heavily on an address on Maitland entitled "The Historical Spirit Incarnate," which I gave at the annual meeting of the American Historical Association in 1951.

Thanks are due the original publishers of these Maitland writings, the sources of which are more specifically identified in the prefatory notes at the heads of the several chapters.

R. L. S.

Contents

Introduction

During Maitland's lifetime he came to be generally regarded by those best qualified to judge his work as the greatest historian English law had ever known, and in the half century that has passed since his death his stature as a legal historian has not diminished. His writing, however, was not confined to the field of legal history. Whatever its subject, it is permeated with a spirit that is the essence of the historical mind. He has a message for everyone who is interested in history, whether professionally or not and no matter in what branch of history or in what particular subjects. His own interests and the character of his historical materials were such that he was often led to offer opinions on questions to which final answers could not be given, though in doing so he was, characteristically, not opinionated. It is not surprising that some of his views have been disputed by other scholars, in his own day and since. But his writings retain their power to stimulate and inspire, even where later investigations, not a few of them stemming from ideas which he himself threw out, have made it necessary to qualify opinions that he advanced. What a distinguished historian of our day, Sir Frank Stenton, has said about one of his books could be said equally well of others, that "the vitality of Maitland's writing, the acuteness of his mind and above all the interest which he could impart to the austerest of technical problems, have made *Domesday Book and Beyond* a source of inspiration which is hardly affected by changes of opinion about its subject-matter." The extent and variety of his historical output seem the more remarkable in view of the brevity of his career as a professional historian—it lasted little more than twenty years—and the fact that much of his time and energy during that short period was consumed in the performance of academic duties. In a bibliography compiled by one of his warm admirers and published soon after his death (A. L. Smith, *Frederic William Maitland: Two Lectures and a Bibliography*) there are listed more than one hundred thirty items, including the books he wrote, the volumes of legal records and other source materials he edited, with introductions which in many cases amount to historical treatises, articles he contributed to various journals, and some of his book reviews.

Maitland was a lawyer, and he is generally thought of, and rightly so, as primarily a historian of English law. But law was not the earliest of his intellectual pursuits. His habits of thought were not formed in the discipline of legal study, which, as law has been taught and learned, has not been calculated to develop a historical mind. He gave evidence of historical interests before he became a lawyer, and it would be a mistake to think of him as essentially a lawyer who just happened to become interested in the history of his subject. He was, rather, what his friend and collaborator Sir Frederick Pollock called him, "a man with a genius for history, who turned its light upon law because law, being his profession, came naturally into the field." One of Maitland's students at Cambridge was George Macaulay Trevelyan, who was to become perhaps the most popular historian of his day in England. He has told us that Maitland used medieval law as a tool to "open . . . the mind of medieval man and to reveal the nature and growth of his institutions." Maitland was a potential historian who became temporarily, and not very willingly it would seem, a practicing lawyer.

Maitland was born in London on May 28, 1850, and died at Las Palmas in the Canary Islands on December 19, 1906. He was the only son, and the youngest in a family of three children, of John Gorham and Emma (Daniell) Maitland. His mother died in 1851, his father in 1863, and he and his sisters were brought up by an aunt, his mother's sister. He came of distinguished forebears; his father and both his grandfathers appear in that British hall of fame, the *Dictionary of National Biography*. His father, a fellow of Trinity College, Cambridge, became a lawyer but left legal practice for the civil service. His maternal grandfather, John Frederic Daniell, was a fellow of the Royal Society and professor of natural science at King's College, London. More should be said about his paternal grandfather, who undoubtedly had very considerable influence upon his historical thought and methods.

Samuel Roffey Maitland, like his son and grandson after him, was a student at Trinity College, Cambridge, was called to the bar, and did not remain long in legal practice. But unlike them, he took holy orders and became Librarian to the Archbishop of Canterbury at Lambeth Palace, London, a position which has been held by several famous historians, William Stubbs and John Richard Green among them. He retired to his small estate in Gloucestershire, where he studied and wrote history and where his grandson as a boy visited him from time to time. At his death, in 1866, this property passed to Frederic William, who came to be known in the county as "Squire Maitland."

The principal writings of the elder Maitland, like those of his grandson, are in the field of medieval history, and there are striking resemblances between the two as historians. Both show a strong historical sense, a strong feeling for the general cultural context in which medieval institutions were embedded and a keen awareness of differences between it and the cultural milieu of their own times, and both are therefore repelled by anachronism. Both are distinctly critical in handling historical evidence and therefore skeptical in their attitude toward historical traditions. Neither is content to stop short of the most reliable original sources available for historical knowledge. In a preface to a volume entitled *The Dark Ages* Samuel Roffey Maitland speaks well of medieval monasticism, but its merits in its own day were not, to his mind, a valid reason for reviving the monastic system in nineteenth-century England, as had recently been proposed. He did not believe that the *medieval* monastic system could be revived. "It seems to me," he writes, "that we can no more revive the Monastic System than the Feudal System. We cannot recall the days of ancient republicanism, or medieval chivalry. . . ." The attempt to do so would be as anachronistic as if "the Duke of Wellington should go down to the house [of lords] in complete armour, or if Julius Caesar should tread the stage in a field-marshal's uniform." The past in the present and the present in the past were equally anachronistic and therefore equally distasteful to him. The elder Maitland lived long before the term "historical relativism" had been coined, but in his historical outlook he was a thorough relativist. He perceived clearly that the institutions of the past could be understood only when viewed in their context, and he knew also that a nineteenth-century man, even a historian, could not become absolutely and consistently medieval.

A letter of Maitland's, written to one of his sisters in 1891, shows his appreciation of his grandfather's critical method in testing historical evidence:

> Judging him merely as I should judge any other literary man, I think him great. It seems to me that he did what was wanted just at the moment when it was wanted and so has a distinct place in the history of history in England. *The Facts and Documents*[1] is the book that I admire most. . . . One has still to do for legal history something of the work which S. R. M. did for ecclesiastical history—to teach men, e.g., that some statement about the thirteenth century does not become the truer because it has been constantly repeated, that "a chain of testimony" is never stronger than its first link. It is the "method" that I admire in S. R. M. more even than the style or the matter—the application to remote events of those canons of evidence which we should all use about affairs of the present day. . . .[2]

At Eton, which he entered in 1863, young Frederic did not distinguish himself in study or in play. He was not attracted to the classics, Greek as it was taught seems to have been actually repulsive to him, and history was not then a recognized study in the

---

[1] *Facts and Documents illustrative of the History, Doctrine, and Rites of the ancient Albigenses & Waldenses.* By the Rev. S. R. Maitland, London, 1832.

[2] H. A. L. Fisher, *Frederic William Maitland: A Biographical Sketch,* Cambridge, 1910, pp. 2–3.

English "public schools." In 1869 he followed his father and grandfather to Trinity College, where his earliest interests—athletics, music, and mathematics—had no obvious relation to what was to become his lifework. Before long, however, he came under the influence of the celebrated Cambridge philosopher Henry Sidgwick, a man of many interests, with results important for his intellectual growth; he later called Sidgwick "one of the acutest, profoundest and most influential thinkers of our time." He read widely in various branches of philosophy, won a scholarship at Trinity, and in 1872 came out at the head of what was called the Moral and Mental Science Tripos. He acquired a reputation as a humorous and brilliant talker and an effective public speaker and already, as an undergraduate, gave more than a hint of that flair for pointing an argument with an epigram that was to characterize his writing and lecturing in after years.

Though Maitland entered Lincoln's Inn, an ancient and famous English law school, in 1872, before his graduation from Cambridge in the following year, the practice of law was not his earliest choice for a profession. While an undergraduate he seems to have been attracted to an academic career. He became much interested in the history of political theory and competed for a Trinity College fellowship with a long essay, "A Historical Sketch of Liberty and Equality as Ideals of English Political

Philosophy from the Time of Hobbes to the Time of Coleridge." [8] Had he won the fellowship, it seems doubtful that he would have become a lawyer. The essay, his earliest substantial piece of historical writing, foreshadows some of his later traits as a historian. It shows in the young scholar, still in his early twenties, a vivid historical sense, a critical faculty, and an interest in legal concepts and in changes which had taken place in them.

Having acquired a thorough training in English law at Lincoln's Inn, he was called to the bar in 1876 and practiced law thereafter for several years, specializing in conveyancing. His familiarity with that highly technical branch of law served him well in his later interpretation of early English land deeds and charters, and afterwards, speaking as a historian, he attached great importance to legal training for anyone who aspired to do good work in legal history. In the law chambers of Benjamin Bickley Rogers, who is still remembered in classical circles for the translations of the comedies of Aristophanes with which he beguiled his leisure hours, the young barrister worked as a conveyancer, and Rogers' reminiscent testimony is eloquent as to his legal talents: ". . . he had not been with me a week before I found that I had in my chambers such a lawyer as I had never met before . . . his opinions, had he

[8] Privately printed in 1875; reprinted in *The Collected Papers of Frederic William Maitland*, ed. by H. A. L. Fisher, 3 vols., Cambridge, 1911, I, 1–161.

suddenly been made a judge, would have been an honor to the Bench." Rogers expressed doubt, however, whether Maitland would have made a professional success as a barrister: ". . . he was the most retiring and diffident man I ever knew; not the least shy or awkward . . . but he was the last man to put himself forward in any way."[4] Maitland himself seems to have shared this doubt. Sir Paul Vinogradoff, the Russian medievalist who became a professor at Oxford, in an obituary article on his long-time friend, recalled Maitland's saying to him when they first met, in 1884, that he "would much rather devote his life to the historical study of English law than watch in his chambers . . . for the footsteps of the client who never comes."[5]

At any rate, Maitland's principal interest in law was in its history rather than its practice. He began a translation, never completed, of the famous work of the German legal historian Friedrich Karl Savigny, *Geschichte des Römischen Rechts,* and hoped to be able to do for English law what Savigny had done for Roman law. He later said that his interest in legal history was first aroused by Frederick Pollock, who became his intimate friend and collaborator. Pollock was a few years older than Maitland and preceded him by a few years in the educational procession—at Eton, Trinity College, and

[4] Fisher, *op. cit.,* pp. 15–17.

[5] "Frederic William Maitland," *English Historical Review,* XXII, 280–281.

Lincoln's Inn. The two friends collaborated in writing the great treatise which quickly became a classic in English legal history, *The History of English Law before the Time of Edward I*, published in two volumes in 1895 and commonly cited as "Pollock and Maitland." The order in which the authors' names appeared on the title page was in accordance with professional legal usage, the order of seniority at the bar. But a note by Pollock, appended to the preface, records that Maitland's share in the work, both in research and in composition, was by far the greater.[6]

It seems evident that Maitland was not really happy in legal practice. He came to perceive clearly a fundamental difference between the legal mind and the historical mind. Many lawyers have written history, and often sadly distorted history. The time-honored method of studying law, in English inns of court and American law schools, has had for its aim, of course, the training of lawyers, not of historians. The lawyer is concerned with precedents, to be sure, but not with the context of his precedents. If, to quote some penetrating words that have been ascribed to the late Thomas Reed Powell, professor of American constitutional law at Columbia and Harvard, who devoted himself to the study of how

[6] In a letter to Justice Holmes of the U. S. Supreme Court (Aug. 23, 1895) Pollock tells how small his share was: only the introduction (not quite all), the chapter on Anglo-Saxon law, and the bulk of the chapter on the early history of contract. *Holmes-Pollock Letters*, I, 60–61.

judges think, "If you think that you can think about a thing inextricably attached to something else, without thinking of the thing it is attached to, then you have a legal mind." The historical mind, on the other hand, sees past events in their contemporary contexts. In his inaugural lecture as Downing Professor of the Laws of England at Cambridge, delivered in 1888 and entitled "Why the History of English Law is not Written," [7] Maitland contrasted the two types of mind:

> A lawyer finds on his table a case about rights of common which sends him to the Statute of Merton. But is it really the law of 1236 that he wants to know? No, it is the ultimate result of the interpretations set on the statute by the judges of twenty generations. The more modern the decision, the more valuable for his purpose. That process by which old principles and old phrases are charged with a new content, is from the lawyer's point of view an evolution of the true intent and meaning of the old law; from the historian's point of view it is almost of necessity a process of perversion and misunderstanding.

While in legal practice Maitland came to be extremely dissatisfied with the state of the branch of English law in which he had specialized, and in his earliest contribution to legal literature, an article on "The Law of Real Property," published in the *Westminster Review* in 1879 (reprinted in *Collected Papers,* I, 162–201), he expressed extreme contempt

[7] See below, pp. 132-144.

for it as being burdensome, vexatious, complicated, unreasonable, and full of anachronistic survivals. He wrote this article as an advocate of radical law reform, not as a legal historian, but a legal historian of our day has seen evidence in it that he "was already at heart a historian." [8]

Law reform was one of Maitland's abiding interests, though he did not write extensively on the subject. It was his mature opinion, expressed near the end of his life, that historical-mindedness, far from being the handmaid of conservatism, is the natural ally of rational reform. It seemed to him that "anyone who really possesses what has been called the historic sense must . . . dislike to see a rule or an idea unfitly surviving in a changed environment," that "anachronism should offend not only his reason, but his taste." [9] He was spiritually akin to the great English law reformers of the early nineteenth century, and he could use equally vigorous language: "One of the primary functions of a legislature is, I conceive, to sweep into the dust-bin the rubbish that inevitably accumulates in the course of legal history." He belongs in what Sir William Holdsworth, author of a multivolume history of English law and an ardent admirer of Maitland, called the "long series of judges, conveyancers, and legislators" whose efforts led to drastic reforms in

---

[8] T. F. T. Plucknett, "Maitland's View of Law and History," *Law Quarterly Review*, vol. 67, p. 184.

[9] *Collected Papers*, III, 486.

English property law in the 1920's. He was ever a sworn foe of what he called "out-worn theories and obsolescent ideas," but his historical sense prevented him from making the crude mistake of condemning theories or ideas in the past because they later became encumbrances and impediments. In connection with the law of real property he spoke of the need for clearing up what he called "that great medieval muddle which passes under the name of feudalism," but he never expressed contempt for feudalism in feudal times.

Writings of Maitland's in the early 1880's show that the dissatisfied legal practitioner was moving into the domain of legal history. Articles came from his pen on subjects far remote from the professional concerns of a nineteenth-century English barrister—articles on the kindred and the blood feud in the ancient laws of Wales, on the criminal liability of the hundred, on the history of malice aforethought.[10] By 1883 he seems to have been ready to give up legal practice, for in that year he became a candidate for the position of Reader in Law at Oxford. But again, as in his competition for the Cambridge fellowship, he was unsuccessful. The year 1884 was to bring fairer prospects.

For one thing, a lasting friendship of importance in his career began in that year. He was a member of an informal group of walking enthusiasts who

[10] Published in *Law Magazine and Review* and reprinted in *Collected Papers,* Vol. I.

called themselves "The Sunday Tramps," begun in 1879 by Leslie Stephen and a few congenial spirits, including Pollock. (Maitland became a welcome guest at Stephen's home, and in 1886 he married Florence Henrietta Fisher, a niece of Mrs. Stephen, a daughter of Herbert Fisher, a judge, and a sister of H. A. L. Fisher, who became a figure of considerable importance in Liberal politics and a historian.[11]) In January, 1884, Vinogradoff, then in England in search of unpublished historical materials, happened to join the "Tramps" as a guest on one of their walks, and he and Maitland met, corresponded thereafter, and became close friends. Vinogradoff was greatly impressed by the wealth of unexploited materials for medieval English legal history in the early plea rolls (records of judicial cases) in the Public Record Office in London and may have talked enthusiastically on this subject to Maitland at their first meeting.[12] At any rate, Maitland's first impor-

---

[11] Maitland later took time off from legal history to write *The Life and Letters of Leslie Stephen*, published in 1906, the last year of Maitland's life. It was a labor of love.

[12] Several years later, in a letter to Vinogradoff (Nov. 15, 1891), Maitland wrote, very likely with some exaggeration: "I often think what an extraordinary piece of luck for me it was that you and I met upon a 'Sunday tramp.' That day determined the rest of my life." Quoted in Fisher, *op. cit.*, p. 51. In this memoir of his brother-in-law Fisher gave currency to a story that it was at a decisive meeting of Vinogradoff and Maitland at Oxford on May 11, 1884, that the latter first learned from the Russian scholar about the plea rolls and that he was thereby inspired to make his first visit to the Public

tant contribution to the history of English law was published in the autumn of 1884—his *Pleas of the Crown for the County of Gloucester*,[13] which he dedicated to Vinogradoff. His introduction shows traits and attitudes and interests that were to characterize his later historical work. It gives evidence of his vigorous historical sense, ever alert to the distorting results of after-mindedness, of his imaginative critical faculty in dealing with historical records, of his appreciation of the value in historical exposition of concrete details and illustrative examples, and of his concern with questions which he was later to explore more fully.

For another reason, too, 1884 stands out in Maitland's career, for in that year he finally abandoned legal practice and committed himself to academic life and professional historianship. He accepted a readership in English law at Cambridge, recently endowed by Sidgwick. Four years later he was elected Downing Professor of the Laws of England, and he held this chair for the rest of his life.

Vinogradoff's study of the medieval English manor led him to Bracton's *De Legibus Angliae*, the most famous treatise on English law written

---

Record Office. This story has been shown to be mythical; it has been established that Maitland worked on plea rolls at the Public Record Office *before* May 11, 1884. See Plucknett, *op. cit.*, *Law Quarterly Review*, vol. 67, pp. 185–187; also F. M. Powicke, *Modern Historians and the Study of History*, p. 10, footnote.

[13] See below, pp. 118ff.

during the Middle Ages. In a letter to *The Athenaeum*, published on July 19, 1884, he called public attention to a manuscript in the Library of the British Museum, written about the middle of the thirteenth century and containing a collection of court cases which he believed, for reasons which he set forth, to have been compiled for Bracton and annotated by him or under his direction; and he urged that the manuscript be published. Maitland acted on this recommendation, with the result that *Bracton's Note Book* was published in 1887 in three volumes under his editorship, with a long introduction which is in itself a substantial historical treatise. Always scrupulous in acknowledging indebtedness, he gave Vinogradoff the entire credit for perceiving the value of the British Museum manuscript for the history of English law. *Bracton's Note Book* established Maitland's reputation as a legal historian.

As a lecturer Maitland made an impression on those who heard him. He was illuminating, notably suggestive and stimulating in what he had to say, which was carefully prepared, and humorous, even at times dramatic, in his way of saying it. Students spoke of his power to create historical atmosphere and make dead bones live. He could convey, at any rate to some of them, his enthusiasm for the subject on which he was lecturing. One of these was James T. Shotwell, afterwards a distinguished professor of history and international relations at Columbia, who knew him in his later years. Shotwell has thus recorded his impressions:

> Maitland lectured on English law . . . as though he were some saintly medieval monk reciting the miracles of his order. His tall gaunt figure was restless with animation; his voice would . . . pass into a sort of liturgic rhythm as he completed his outline of some large cycle of legal development. . . . Yet even at a moment of what seemed genuine enthusiasm, . . . a sudden shaft of humor would flash into the lecture, and, though the tense face hardly relaxed, the eyes in an instant were all play. . . . Few of his students took notes. The lecture was too interesting.[14]

In addition to formal lectures he used to give informal instruction to small groups of students—seminars we would call them, I suppose—in medieval handwriting and shorthand (paleography) and in the reading of medieval charters and other kinds of documents (diplomatics).

In 1887 the Selden Society was founded for the purpose of advancing the knowledge of English law by publishing firsthand materials for the study of its history. Maitland was the prime mover in its establishment and later became its literary director. The society published twenty-one volumes during his lifetime, of which six were edited by him alone, two by him in collaboration, and the others, some of them undertaken at his suggestion, underwent his editorial supervision. His last major enterprise was an edition

[14] *Political Science Quarterly*, XXII, 288.

of the Year Books (law reports) of the reign of Edward II,[15] three volumes of which he lived to see through the press.

After all the argument and controversy that have taken place in historical and historico-philosophical circles concerning the uses and aims of historical study, the nature of historical knowledge, and that tempting apple of discord, historical relativism—and the literature thereon is voluminous—historians still speak respectfully about historical truth, when they speak about it at all. Only a selfless dedication to the pursuit of truth could have sustained labors so laborious and pains so painful as those to which Maitland subjected himself. A single example will serve for illustration. Toward the end of his life, when he had reason to believe that not many more years were left, he turned from a continuation of "Pollock and Maitland," which he had much at heart, to the preparation of a critical edition of early Year Books, because he regarded this latter as an indispensable preliminary to the former. To an understanding of the Year Books, however, there was also an indispensable preliminary—a thorough knowledge of the language in which they were written, the Anglo-French used in law courts in England in the thirteenth and fourteenth centuries. So he turned grammarian, orthographer, and phoneticist. For the competence with which he performed this exacting task we have the testimony of a distinguished con-

[15] See below, pp. 231ff.

temporary French philologist, Paul Meyer, who recommended Maitland's laborious excursion into medieval law French (published in the introduction to the first volume of the Year Books of Edward II which he edited for the Selden Society) to all students of Old French in any of its varieties. Maitland's achievement seems all the more remarkable in that he was not a trained philologist, and that his work on the Year Books was done under the severe handicap of enforced absences from England. By 1899 it had become clear that for reasons of health he should no longer live there during the winter months, and his remaining winters were spent in milder climates, all but one of them in the Canary Islands. He retained to the last the strength to endure the drudgery involved in the most exacting type of scholarship. He knew that errors are made, almost inevitably, in the quest for knowledge, and for the honest mistakes of historians he had all due charity. But the exposure of intentional falsification he considered to be a very pleasant duty. In reviewing a volume on English law books compiled in the early twelfth century he said: "To watch Dr. Liebermann tracking a forger from fraud to fraud will be a delight to every well-constituted mind." [16] The pursuit of historical truth was Maitland's ruling passion, and it explains most of his traits as a historian.

Anyone who has read more than a very little of

[16] *English Historical Review*, IX, 742.

Maitland will be impressed, as all students of his writings have been, by his concreteness and attention to detail. He had a healthy distrust of the glittering generality that disdains illustration. "People can't understand old law," he once remarked, "unless you give a few concrete illustrations; at least I can't." In the introduction to his *Pleas of the Crown for the County of Gloucester* he says that "a large stock of examples, given with all their concrete details, may serve to produce a body of flesh and blood for the ancient rules which . . . are apt to seem abstract, unreal, impracticable." His writings are alive with the doings of men, even though the men must sometimes be left unnamed. He never forgot that laws and institutions and ideas have no existence, no life and evolution of their own, apart from human beings. In his obituary article on Maitland, Vinogradoff wrote: "Although his work never stuck in details for their own sake, it will always remain an example of what a thorough grasp of details and keen investigation of all the particulars of a case can mean in the research of scientific truth."

Maitland, however, was not bogged down in detail and incapable of generalization. The combination of broad views and minute investigation, of what Macaulay called landscape painting and map making in the writing of history, is one of his marked characteristics. Generalization is not confined to surveys of wide scope that he wrote, such as his masterly summary of the results of research which was published as a preliminary chapter in the second edition of "Pollock and Maitland" and entitled "The Dark Age in Legal History," and his article on the history of English law, published in the eleventh edition of the *Encyclopaedia Britannica.* It is much in evidence in his technical writings also, sometimes in epigrammatic remarks which drive points home and clinch arguments. These are never mere purple patches, sewn on just for ornament.

Though primarily a legal historian, Maitland was not a narrowly legal historian. His major specialty was the history of the English common law, but the common law did not develop in isolation from other bodies of law, from equity, for example, administered in the Court of Chancery, and from canon law, administered in the ecclesiastical courts, and he was led to study the history of these other legal systems. Nor was his curiosity confined to the domain of legal history as a whole. He realized that specialization, division of labor, is necessary for the advancement of knowledge, but no historian has perceived more clearly that the various departments into which the whole of history, *considered as knowledge about the past,* has been divided for convenience and utility are not severally self-sufficient or self-explanatory. No historian has felt more sensitively that this departmentalization of knowledge does not correspond to anything in history, *considered as the flow of events in the past,* to anything inherent in the historic process itself—that it tends, on the contrary, to obscure relationships which have always existed in that process as an undivided whole. For Maitland there was nothing sacrosanct about the boundaries of the various departments of history, and they ought not to be thought of as barriers. He counted it for righteousness in his friend Leslie Stephen that he was "a great contemner of boundaries, whom no scheme of the sciences, no delimitation of departments, would keep in the highway if he had a mind to go across country." Maitland knew that the historian of law should often visit other historical bailiwicks—the economic, social, religious, political, for example—for enlightenment and explanation, and, conversely, that specialists in other historical domains ought on occasion to cross the frontiers of legal history.

In the formative period of his mental life Maitland read widely in different branches of philosophy, but the bent of his mind was historical, and perhaps he was too essentially and wholeheartedly the historian to take very kindly to the philosophy of history. His writings, at any rate, may be searched in vain, I believe, for references to so-called historical laws, determinism of any variety (providential, economic, racial, geographic, or any other), controlling social forces, or *Zeitgeister*. He did not misspend time and energy in the attempt to establish "fundamental causes." He knew that causation in history is always multiple and complex and that among historical antecedents there are always events that look like historical accidents, events which it seems impossible to account for as even probable results of *their* known antecedents. He never brushed aside as vain or useless conjectures as to what might have happened if some preceding occurrence had not occurred, never condemned conjectures on the part of historians in response to hypothetical questions contrary to historical facts. Without such conjectures, indeed, it would seem to be impossible to estimate the significance of events and personalities in history, and he himself at times engaged in them. For example, in a passage in "Pollock and Maitland" dealing with the results of the Norman Conquest in English legal history he asks whether a charter of liberties would ever have been granted in England if William the Conqueror had left only one son. And again, in his *English Law and the Renaissance,*[17] when he is speaking of what he regarded as England's narrow escape from a "reception" of Roman law in the middle years of the sixteenth century, he says that "if there had been a Reception—well, I have not the power to guess and you have not the time to hear what would have happened; but I think that we should have had to rewrite a great deal of history."

Maitland's mind, like those of other great historians, was of strongly critical cast. The exercise of private judgment, which made him in religion a dissenter from dissent, became early an integral part of the man, and a right which was a necessity for him

[17] See below, pp. 106ff.

in his own mental life he assumed to be a right of others. He took no false pride in his own opinions and welcomed criticism of them. In the estimation of H. A. L. Fisher, who knew him both as man and as historian, "no one was more entirely free from self-importance or from any desire to defend, after they had become untenable, positions which he had once been inclined to maintain." He was forever asking himself questions, nor was his curiosity confined to matters of obvious importance. An inconspicuous "&c." in the title of English sovereigns gave rise to an article which showed that what looked trivial on the surface originated in a deliberate stroke of statesmanship.[18] Maitland's ingenuity and imaginative power in textual criticism are widely in evidence in his writings, notably in his editions of documentary materials. Impressive illustrations can be found in his introduction to the Selden Society's edition of *The Mirror of Justices.*[19] This was a medieval law book, or what purported to be such, which enjoyed a high reputation from the days of Sir Edward Coke in the seventeenth century to the nineteenth century. It does not seem to have been a success in its own day or in the Middle Ages generally. It was not printed until 1642. In some way Coke, who died in 1634, acquired a manuscript copy of the book which, says Maitland, he devoured with his habitual "uncritical voracity" and pronounced

[18] See below, pp. 252ff.
[19] See below, pp. 204ff.

to be "a very ancient and learned treatise of the laws and usages of this Kingdom." He incorporated in his *Institutes* many stories that he had found in this book, and since generations of English lawyers were brought up on Coke's *Institutes, The Mirror of Justices* passed into English legal tradition as a great authority. Maitland was not the first to cast doubts on its reliability, but he went much further in that direction than earlier critics had gone. His object was to find out from internal evidence when and why the book was written and what kind of book it was. His discussion of these questions is a first-rate illustration of historical detective work combined with flights of imagination.

Independence of judgment brought Maitland at times into conflict with opinions and schools of thought which were widely accepted and had the support of great names. A case in point resulted from a study that he made of Roman canon law in English ecclesiastical courts in the Middle Ages, the results of which are set forth in his *Roman Canon Law in the Church of England* (1898). He came to conclusions contrary to the opinion held by the High Anglican party in the Church of England, which enjoyed the approval of the great Stubbs and the endorsement of a Royal Commission on Ecclesiastical Courts in a report made in 1883. According to this view Roman canon law, or papal law, had not been binding on ecclesiastical courts in medieval England unless accepted by the church in England.

This was, as Pollock remarked, "a patriotic, a comfortable and, above all, an anti-Roman doctrine. . . ." Vinogradoff called it "a kind of ante-dated Anglicanism." Maitland came to the opposite opinion, namely, that papal canons were treated by the English ecclesiastical courts as being, of their own force, binding law. Bishop Stubbs himself was convinced by Maitland's arguments. Yet Maitland, though not overawed by great names, was not polemical by preference. He did not seek controversy or rejoice in it, like some of his predecessors, contemporaries, and successors. He wrote many book reviews, in which there was much constructive criticism, but petty faultfinding was distasteful to him. He disliked it in others and never practiced it himself; he was habitually considerate toward other scholars. His historical criticisms, according to Vinogradoff, exemplified the maxim *suaviter in modo, fortiter in re.* Only if he thought that injustice had been done did he show signs of strong feeling, and then he could be devastating. A good example of this is his shattering refutation of an ill-advised and unfair attack which Sir Henry Maine, a renowned jurist and historian, had made on Bracton.[20]

Maitland was skillful in summarizing the results of research in attractive form, and some of his writing was intended for the general public that takes some interest in history, but the writings that best exhibit his historical genius were addressed to more

[20] See below, pp. 198ff.

specialized classes of readers. Though he was devoid of the intellectual snobbishness that prizes knowledge the more when it is esoteric, it would be correct to call him a historian's historian rather than a general reader's historian. He was eager to advance learning and to aid other scholars and encourage them to labor, not in *his* vineyard (for no historian could be less monopolistic or proprietary in his attitude toward his field of specialization) but in the vineyard with him. His perception of historical problems awaiting solution and of work that needed to be done in aid of historical scholarship made him extraordinarily fertile in suggestion. He not only made great contributions to historical knowledge by his own investigations but also stimulated others to make further contributions by theirs. He regarded it a crime against history for the historian to eliminate from his finished product, in the name of art, the evidences and processes of reasoning on which it had been based. He spoke with playful sarcasm of England as a land "where men are readily persuaded that hard labour is disagreeable and the signs of hard labour are disgusting." He gave high praise to historians who took their readers into their confidence and showed them historianship behind the scenes. Of Bishop Stubbs he said: "No other Englishman has so completely displayed to the world the whole business of the historian from the winning of the raw material to the narrating and generalising." Like Stubbs he was a mighty contributor to historical knowledge, and a historical editor who carried the editorial art to its highest levels. No other series of introductions to historical sources deserves to be placed above theirs.

That Maitland's appeal has not been to the general reading public is explained largely, no doubt, by the nature of his subject matter. The historian of ideas and institutions—and this essentially is what he was—has never enjoyed the popular favor accorded to the narrative historian. "The History of Institutions cannot be mastered—can scarcely be approached—without an effort." Such is the majestic sentence with which Stubbs began the preface to his *Constitutional History of England.* One cannot imagine *Domesday Book and Beyond* displacing the latest best-selling novel on dressing tables in young ladies' boudoirs, the ambition that Macaulay cherished for his *History of England.* The kind of history to which Maitland devoted his best efforts requires for its appreciation more active response on the reader's part, greater mental exertion, and a higher degree of sympathetic imagination than the metallic rhetoric of Macaulay or the glowing prose of John Richard Green. It is also, as Maitland perceived, more risky than narrative history. "Would Gibbon's editor," he asked, "find so few mistakes to rectify if Gibbon had seriously tried to make his readers live for a while under the laws of Franks and Lombards?"

Maitland, however, conclusively refutes the

notion, widespread though it seems to be, that there is some kind of incompatibility between deep learning and good writing, for he was a master in the expression of thought in English prose. Contemporaries who were familiar with his writings were impressed by his literary qualities and noted his gift for making unpromising subjects interesting. A generation after his death the editors of a collection of his articles coupled what they called "the matchless attraction of his style" with "the brilliant scholarship and originality of thought which he brought to bear upon every topic that he handled." [21] He had no set method, nor any single manner, of writing. He was eloquent (though never pompous) or homely (though never vulgar) or gay (though never flippant) as his subject or his mood moved him. He was interested in words, took them seriously, chose them with care, and liked to manipulate them. Humor is a salient trait in his writing, humor "abounding in delightful surprises," says Pollock, "overflowing even into the titles of learned papers, breaking out in footnotes with rapid allusive touches." Vinogradoff speaks of "the wealth of humour that pervaded all his writings, in spite of their severe aims and their highly technical details." An example of the kind of refreshment that the reader gets in Maitland's technical papers occurs in an article on "The Corporation Sole," in which, having occasion to speak of

[21] *Maitland: Selected Essays,* ed. by H. D. Hazeltine, G. Lapsley, and P. H. Winfield (1936), p. vii.

a gift of land "to God and the church of St. Peter of Westminster," he remarks, "We observe that God and St. Peter are impracticable feoffees." [22] There were darts of sarcasm and irony in his quiver, and he knew how to discharge them with telling effect, but his darts, however pointed, were never poisoned, and they were rarely aimed at individuals. His writings are full of epigrammatic phrases and remarks. He often made use of analogy and metaphor, though recognizing that they are often misleading and generally unsafe as a basis for argument. Maitland is not always crystal clear. He often had to deal with ideas that were indefinite and hazy and with facts that were complicated, and it is one of his merits as a historian that he does not make them seem clear and simple. He knew that overdefiniteness and oversimplification are faults in a historian. Some of the classical expositions of "the feudal system" and "the manorial system" are likely to make medieval society look simpler than it was, but, he said, "we think it part of our duty to insist that the facts which the lawyers of the thirteenth century had to bring within their theories were complicated." [23] Hazy ideas and complicated facts are not the easiest subject matter for lucid exposition. Then there are difficulties in expounding technical matters, and much of Maitland's writing is technical. But these considerations apart, he seems some-

[22] *Collected Papers*, III, 229.

[23] Pollock and Maitland, 2d ed., 1898, I, 296.

times to be unduly allusive, occasionally even intentionally inexplicit, perhaps because he assumes too much knowledge on the part of his readers.

During the entire course of man's thinking and talking and writing about the past of his species, throughout what has been called "the history of history," conditions and events of later times have cast their shadows behind them. This after-mindedness, to give it a short name, has usually been present-mindedness and has been through the ages the most potent breeder of anachronism, the most persistent cause of historical distortion. If Francis Bacon had lived in our times instead of the seventeenth century, he might have included it among those "idols" on which he discoursed in his *Novum Organum*, those false notions and erroneous conceptions, deeply embedded in the human mind, which impede the advance of knowledge. Its antithesis is, let us call it, historical-mindedness, which sees, or tries to see, past events and ideas and institutions in their contemporary context. Historical-mindedness, in this sense, was alien to prevailing habits of thought before belief in evolution came to condition thinking about the past, and acceptance of the philosophy of evolution did not become widespread before the nineteenth century. Once in a while before then a voice had been raised against after-mindedness, but it was a voice crying in the wilderness. In England there was Sir Henry Spelman, for example, an early seventeenth-century historian (in the days when historians used to be called "antiquaries") of remarkable learning, considering the resources available to him, and of great originality, whose main interests were in English legal and ecclesiastical history. In the opening paragraph of a tract entitled *Of Parliaments* Spelman took occasion to criticize earlier antiquaries for their present-mindedness: "When States are departed from their original Constitution, and that original by tract of time worn out of Memory, the succeeding Ages, viewing what is past by the present, conceive the former to have been like to that they live in; and framing thereupon erroneous Propositions, do likewise make thereon erroneous Inferences and Conclusions." Then, four or five generations after Spelman, there was John Reeves, also a legal historian and also impressed by the prevailing after-mindedness of his predecessors. He said as much in a preface to the first volume of his multivolume *History of the English Law*, published in 1783, and hopefully announced a new plan of his own.[24] Spel-

[24] "I found that modern writers, in discoursing of the antient law, were too apt to speak in modern terms, and generally with a reference to some modern usage. Hence it followed, that what they adduced was too often distorted and misrepresented. . . . As this had a tendency to produce very great mistakes, it appeared to me, that, in order to have a right conception of our old jurisprudence, it would be necessary to forget for a while every alteration which had been made since, to enter upon it with a mind wholly unprejudiced, and to peruse it with the same attention that is bestowed on

man and Reeves, however, like most men who have been "ahead of their times," had little if any effect upon traditional attitudes and points of view.

John Fiske, an enthusiastic devotee of the doctrine of evolution as well as a celebrated American popularizer of history, emphasized the need of freeing the mind from "bondage to the modern map," a phrase which he borrowed from the English historian Edward A. Freeman, in order to understand what the European mariners of the fifteenth and sixteenth centuries were seeking. "The ancient map," he said in the preface to his *Discovery of America*, "must take its place. . . . In dealing with the discovery of America one must steadily keep before one's mind the quaint notions of ancient geographers. . . . It was just these distorted and hazy notions that swayed the minds and guided the movements of the great discoverers." Bondage to the modern map, however, has been only one phase of bondage to the modern in general from which the study and writing of history have suffered so much. The process of emancipation from this bondage needed, and still needs, to be extended to all

---

a system of modern law. The law of the time would then be learned in the language of the time, untinctured with new opinions; and when that was clearly understood, the alterations made therein in subsequent periods might be deduced, and exhibited to the mind of a modern jurist in the true colours in which they appeared to persons who lived in those respective periods." Attention has recently been called to Reeves's forgotten exemplary sentiment by C. H. S. Fifoot in his *Law and History in the Nineteenth Century* (1956).

branches of history—to the history of institutions and ideas no less than the history of geographical discovery. Maitland's clear and steady perception of this need in historiography was, it seems to me, the most distinguishing trait in his historianship. It pervades his writings. A good example is to be found in the introduction to his edition of the roll of one of the later parliaments of Edward I, published in 1893.[25] This was, as a medievalist of our day has called it, "a magnificent attack on after-mindedness." [26] It threw a flood of light on the nature of early parliaments, showing how different they were from parliaments of later times, though scholars were slow to appreciate its importance in parliamentary history.

Historical-mindedness, Maitland early came to realize, is very difficult in the field of early custom and law. It is much harder to find out what our remote ancestors thought—and for him the history of law ought to be a history of ideas—than to find out what implements they made. Speaking of work that had been done in particular phases of legal history—the history of real property law, of criminal law, etc.—he says: "Everywhere the investigator finds himself compelled to deal with ideas which are not the ideas of modern times. These he has painfully to reconstruct, and he cannot do so with-

---

[25] See below, pp. 46ff.

[26] Helen M. Cam, *Selected Historical Essays of F. W. Maitland*, p. xix.

out calling in question much of the traditional learning. . . ."[27] Again and again Maitland tells us, in one connection and another, that the emergence of modern ideas ought not to be antedated, that history ought not to be hurried. "Against many kinds of anachronism we now guard ourselves. We are careful of costume, of armour and architecture, of words and forms of speech. But it is far easier to be careful of these things than to prevent the intrusion of untimely ideas. . . . If, for example, we introduce the *persona ficta* too soon, we shall be doing worse than if we armed Hengist and Horsa with machine guns or pictured the Venerable Bede correcting proofs for the press."[28] In history, as in logic and mathematics, a *reductio ad absurdum* can be effective in refuting a fallacy. "It is reported," Maitland wrote in one of his early book reviews, "that London auctioneers deem no house worthy to be called a 'mansion' unless it has backstairs; therefore, every *mansio* mentioned in any document of the twelfth century must have had backstairs. This may be strange reasoning, but it is hardly stranger than to take a piece of Coke and illustrate Domesday with it."[29]

Again and again, explicitly and implicitly, Maitland warns us against forcing modern ideas on the Middles Ages. The problem in hand may be the

---

[27] *Collected Papers*, II, 8.

[28] *Domesday Book and Beyond*, p. 356.

[29] *English Historical Review*, III, 569.

status of the *servus* of Domesday Book. Was he thought of as a thing or as a person—or as neither? "We may well doubt," says Maitland, "whether this principle—'The slave is a thing, not a person'—can be fully understood by a grossly barbarous age. It implies the idea of a person, and in the world of sense we find not persons but men." [30] Modern legal conceptions are in general too definite, modern legal distinctions too sharply drawn, to suit medieval facts. "As we go backwards the familiar outlines become blurred; the ideas become fluid, and instead of the simple we find the indefinite." [31] Thus in modern law a sharp distinction is drawn between a corporation and a group of co-owners. But "we may suspect . . . that in a remote past these two very different notions, namely, that of land owned by a corporation and that of land owned by a group of co-owners, were intimately blent in some much vaguer notion that was neither exactly the one nor exactly the other. . . ." [32] Again, a sharp distinction has been drawn by modern historians between "alodial ownership" and "feudal tenure," but it ought not to be pushed too far back for, in the eleventh century, as Maitland pointed out, men were said to hold land of others *in alodio*. "To whatever quarter we look, the law [in the late thirteenth century] seems to be emerging into clearness out of

---

[30] See below, p. 96.

[31] *Ibid.*

[32] *Domesday Book and Beyond*, p. 341.

a confused and contentious past. The courts are drawing a line between franchises and feudal rights; but it is no easy task, and violence must be done to the facts and the theories of former times." [33]

Maitland knew that after-mindedness is not an exclusively modern phenomenon. He knew that men in *all* ages had trodden that primrose path which has always led to anachronism and distortion of *earlier* ages. Medieval lawyers, in whose thinking he was especially interested, were thoroughly after-minded, as was shown, for example, in the law of villeinage in the thirteenth century—"it seems to betray the handiwork of lawyers who have forced ancient facts into a modern theory."

Domesday Book and Beyond is, as its title suggests, an example of the retrogressive method in history, the method of working back from the later known to the earlier unknown, of which Frederick Seebohm, among English historians, was a conspicuous exponent; and Maitland gave Seebohm high praise for the insights he was able to gain from his method. The question may properly be asked whether this method was consistent with Maitland's teaching against after-mindedness. There was, obviously, a danger that in using Domesday Book to lighten the darkness that lay beyond it, anachronism and distortion would result. He was fully alive to this danger; we have his word for it that "the

[33] *Select Pleas in Manorial and other Seignorial Courts*, Vol. I, Introduction, p. xxiv.

method which would argue from what *is* in one century to what *was* in an earlier century, requires of him who employs it the most circumspect management." [34] He looked upon the retrogressive method as one to be resorted to only for want of a better, only where adequate contemporary evidence was lacking. It was not for him the ideal method. In studying parliamentary history in its beginnings "it is hard to look at the thirteenth century save by looking at it through the distorting medium of the fourteenth," hard but not impossible. "We must judge the [parliament] rolls of Edward I's reign on their own merits without reference to the parliament rolls of his grandson's, or of any later, reign." [35]

"The verdict of history" is a trite phrase, but it is seldom if ever found in Maitland. It has a connotation of finality that is alien to his approach to history. Even in the realm of ethics there are no absolutes for a relativist. Bracton, for example, ought not to be accused of plagiarism because he did not conform to modern standards in acknowledging indebtedness to others. In his time nobody did. "Literary communism" was the order of the day. A contrast may be noted between Maitland and Lord Acton in their conceptions of the attitude toward human behavior in the past appropriate to the historian. The two men were colleagues at

[34] *Collected Papers*, II, 314. Italics mine.

[35] See below, p. 75.

Cambridge, where Acton was Regius Professor of Modern History from 1895 till his death in 1902. There was friendship and mutual respect between them. Acton discussed his plan for the *Cambridge Modern History* with Maitland and invited him to contribute to it, which Maitland did; and Maitland recognized Acton's colossal erudition and wrote an appreciative, though not uncritically laudatory obituary article on him. In his Inaugural Lecture as Regius Professor Acton exhorted his hearers "to try others by the final maxim that governs your own lives, and to suffer no man and no cause to escape the undying penalty which history has the power to inflict on wrong." He paid little heed to what he himself called "the time test," but for Maitland "the time test" was the essential consideration in forming historical judgments about anybody or anything.

Retrojection of the present into the past should be guarded against as far as possible—but how far was it possible?

> If we speak, we must speak with words; if we think, we must think with thoughts. We are moderns, and our words and thoughts can not but be modern. Perhaps, as Mr. Gilbert once suggested, it is too late for us to be early English. Every thought will be too sharp, every word will imply too many contrasts. We must, it is to be feared, use many words and qualify our every statement until we have almost contradicted it.[36]

---

[36] See below, p. 178.

And how "in some yet distant age men will see or fancy that they see the time in which we live, is a question that even the most ignorant of us should not readily answer."[37] The ideal of historical-mindedness, of objectivism, may not be fully attainable, but ought not a man's reach to exceed his grasp? At any rate it did not occur to Maitland to build a philosophy of historiography upon the difference between the two.

A mind as acute as Maitland's, and historically conditioned as his was, could not fail to be constantly concerned with the meanings of words, with ambiguities in their meanings, with changes that have come over their meanings in the course of time. It might seem to be of little historical importance whether in Domesday Book a man was said to hold land under (*sub*) a lord or of (*de*) a lord, but this was not Maitland's view. For an understanding of early English landholding much hinges, he believed, on a distinction between the two Latin prepositions. He tells us that "*sub* lays stress on the lord's power, which may well be of a personal or justiciary, rather than of a proprietary kind, while *de* imports a theory about the origin of the tenure; it makes the tenant's rights look like derivative rights:—it is supposed that he gets his land from his lord."[38] Again, a single word may carry more than a single meaning. *Dominus*, for example, may signify a slaveowner, but

---

[37] *Collected Papers*, III, 438.

[38] See below, pp. 104-105.

it may also mean a feudal suzerain; *dominium* may mean ownership or rule, or a blend of the two.[39]

The problem that lies at the heart of semantics arises from the identification of, or confusion between, the words, the verbal labels, or *symbols*, used for objects, qualities, ideas, and, in general, whatever talk or writing is about, and the objects, qualities, and ideas to which the symbols refer, the *referents*, as semanticists call them. In reality there is, of course, no direct and inherent connection between the word and what it refers to, as Locke was at pains to point out in his *Essay concerning Human Understanding*. A rose by any other name would smell as sweet. But a tacit assumption that a direct connection between symbol and referent actually exists is deeply ingrained in the human mind. Words used as symbols for what is indefinite and vague, for abstractions such as righteousness, justice, liberty, and the like, evoke widely different referents in different minds, and effective communication is thereby impaired, or blocked. Agreement regarding the referent may be called the goal of semantics. Maitland did not employ the vocabulary of semantics, which is not strange since the term itself was only beginning to come into English usage as the name of the science of meaning toward the close of his life. Yet he was a pioneer in what might be called historical semantics, a fertile field which

[39] *Domesday Book and Beyond*, pp. 342–344; Pollock and Maitland, I, 412.

has been only slightly cultivated by historians,[40] though lexicographers, with their obsolete definitions of words, have long been professionally concerned with it.

A vivid appreciation of the instability of meaning attached to many words was one of Maitland's major perceptions. The word *landlord* is an instance in point. "We make one word of it," he remarked, "and throw a strong accent on the first syllable. The lordliness has evaporated; but it was there once. Ownership has come out brightly and intensely; the element of superiority, of government, has vanished." His sensitivity to varying shades of meaning attached to a word is illustrated by the pains he took to show that in Bracton's day the word *manerium* (manor) was not a technical term of law, susceptible of precise definition. As a historian of law he was impressed by the fact that lawyers had taken their terms from popular speech and given them technical meaning and definition. This was the case with the word *seisin*, for example.[41] Sometimes a word continued to have both a technical meaning

[40] Some twenty years ago Walton Hamilton and Douglass Adair wrote a pioneer book in this field entitled *The Power to Govern: The Constitution—Then and Now*. Recent Supreme Court decisions which hinged on the meaning of the words "commerce . . . among the several states" in the Constitution of the United States led the authors to try to find out what the word *commerce* meant to the framers of the Constitution. They made a heroic and impressive attempt to get back to a world that had passed away.

[41] See below, pp. 87ff.

for lawyers and a vaguer meaning for laymen—a source of possible ambiguity.

Maitland did an immense amount of translation, and the way of translators is hard, as he early discovered. How, for instance, ought Latin terms in Domesday Book to be rendered into English?

> If we translate *miles* by *soldier* or *warrior*, this may be too indefinite; if we translate it by *knight*, this may be too definite, and yet leave open the question whether we are comparing the *miles* of 1086 [the year of the Domesday Survey] with the *cniht* of unconquered [i.e., Anglo-Saxon] England or with the knight of the thirteenth century. If we render *vicecomes* by *sheriff*, we are making our sheriff too little of a *vicomte*. When *comes* is before us we have to choose between giving Britanny an *earl*, giving Chester a *count*, or offending some of our *comites* by invidious distinctions.[42]

Nor could the semantic problem be evaded in translating from a modern language. Thoroughly at home in German, which he had learned in childhood and for which he had a strong liking, he sometimes had to be satisfied with the least inadequate English rendering of a German expression. He came to the conclusion that an English translation of the work of a German lawyer could, at best, never be entirely satisfactory: "To take the most obvious instance, his *Recht* is never quite our *Right* or quite our *Law*." Sometimes a German word seemed to him preferable to its not quite equivalent

[42] See below, p. 95.

English counterpart. He was led to speculate on the comparative semantic merits of the German and English languages for legal history. The German historian, he concluded, had at his disposal more clearly defined terms and sharper concepts than the English historian, but this was not an unmitigated advantage for it might lead him to construct theories about early times too sharp to be true. Still he could see possibilities that are "concealed from us in our fluffier language; and the sharp one-sided theory will at least state the problem that is to be solved."

When judged in relation to the state of knowledge and the standards of learning in English legal history when Maitland entered that field, he appears as a towering figure. Personal affection and profound respect did not impair the judgment of Sir Frederick Pollock when he wrote in an obituary article on his old friend and collaborator:

> It is not easy to convey an adequate notion of Maitland's work to those who have not themselves labored in the same field. It is still less easy for any one to appreciate the difficulties or the success who does not remember the conditions under which he started. . . . Looking back some twenty-five years, we see the early history of the Common Law still obscure, insulated, a seeming chaos of technical antiquities. Historians excusably shrank from it, and the lawyers who really knew much of it could almost be counted on one's fingers. . . . This was the world which Maitland's genius transformed. . . . So com-

plete has the transformation been that our children will hardly believe how uncritical their grandfathers were, and on what palpable fictions they were nourished. . . . Maitland commanded the dry bones to live, and henceforth they are alive.

I

Historical-Mindedness

In the reign of Edward I (1272-1307) many petitions to the king, or to the king and his council, were dealt with in meetings, or colloquies, known as parliaments (parliamenta *in the medieval Latin in which the records of early parliaments were written). Maitland's interest in these petitions and in the action taken on them led him to the project of editing an early parliament roll, that of a parliament held in 1305, which had not been previously published in full. The result was a volume, published in 1893 in the Rolls Series, entitled* Records of the Parliament holden at Westminster on the Twenty-Eighth Day of February, in the Thirty-Third Year of the Reign of King Edward the First, *commonly cited by its alternative and less cumbersome title* Memoranda de Parliamento. *Maitland's introduction, from which the following extracts have been taken, came to be recognized as a turning point in parliamentary studies. It threw much light on the relation of early parliaments to the king's council, emphasized their judicial character, and made clear how different they were from parliaments in later times. The presence of magnates or elected representatives, the lords and commons of the future, was not yet essential to the existence of a parliament. "As yet any meeting of the king's council that has been solemnly summoned for general business seems to be a parliament."*

One of the earliest, amplest and most complete of the ancient rolls of parliament has never yet been printed in full. It is the roll of the parliament held by Edward I. in the spring of the year 1305. Somehow or another it wandered away from most of its fellow rolls of the same reign. They, a sadly fragmentary series, were until late years in the Chapter House at Westminster, the treasury of the receipt of the exchequer. The parliament rolls of later reigns were among the chancery records at the Tower of London. Our roll had found a home, and then a sepulchre, in the office of the king's remembrancer.

As a whole it has never been published, but for a long time past many of the entries that are upon it have been known to the world. To explain how this came about, we must go back to the fourteenth century, when someone who had access to the parliamentary records selected from the rolls of the first two Edwards such things as interested him, and had them transcribed into a book. That book still exists. It has borne various names; it has been cited as "Liber Irrotulamentorum de Parliamentis"; it has been called "The Black Book of the Tower"; but probably its best known title is "Vetus Codex." In the sixteenth and seventeenth centuries when lawyers and politicians were beginning to explore the early history of parliament, it did such excellent service that it earned a pre-eminent dignity:—among all ancient manuscripts it was the Vetus Codex.

Now that the as yet unprinted part of the roll ought to be given to the world seemed clear. Our records of the first age of parliamentary history are not so many that we can afford to leave one—and that the handsomest of them all—unstudied. On the other hand there was much to be said against reprinting anything that had already been printed. After long hesitation, however, and divers experiments, I have sought and obtained permission to print here all that is upon the roll, for an opportunity seemed to have offered itself for the accomplishment of a task that has never yet been attempted, namely, the illustration of a good and typical parliament roll by means of those parliamentary petitions which are its ground work.

On the 12th of November 1304 King Edward issued from Burstwick writs for a parliament to be holden at Westminster on the 16th of February 1305. He was on his way back from Scotland. He kept Christmas at Lincoln and was there as late as the 12th of January. On the 22nd he was at Spalding and thence he issued a second set of writs. Events, he said, had happened which made it impossible for him to be at Westminster on the appointed day, so the parliament was postponed to the 28th of February. Slowly and by a circuitous route he travelled southward, for we hear of him at Walsingham, Swaffham, Thetford, Bury St. Edmunds, Exning, Wilbraham, Royston, Braughing, Standon, Wades Hill, Ware, Waltham. On the 26th of January he addressed a letter under his privy seal to the chancellor, which may perhaps explain the postponement. He expected that in the ensuing parliament the clergy would call him in question and he directed that a search should be made in the chancery for any documents which might bear upon the matters in dispute. By other letters under the privy seal, dated on the 5th of February, of which we must speak at greater length hereafter, he directed the appointment of receivers and auditors of petitions; he desired that the petitions should, so far as was possible, be disposed of before his arrival at Westminster. Meanwhile the sheriffs of Kent, Surrey and Sussex had been bidden to send up great quantities of corn and ale to Westminster for the maintenance of the king's household. On the 27th he entered London and stayed at the Hospital of St. Katharine near the Tower. On the 28th the parliament was opened at Westminster.

It was a full parliament in our sense of that term. The three estates of the realm met the king and his council. The great precedent of 1295 had been followed and, if the writs of summons were punctually obeyed, the assembly was a large one. By rights there should have been present some ninety-five prelates, about a hundred and forty-five representatives of the inferior clergy, nine earls (if we include the Prince of Wales and the Earl of Angus), ninety-four barons, seventy-four knights of the shires, and about two hundred citizens and burgesses; altogether some six hundred men. Besides these we must take account of thirty-three members of the king's council to whom writs were sent, and, as we shall see hereafter, there were yet other men present and performing important duties, men who had a special knowledge of Scotland and Gascony.

This assembly was kept together for just three weeks. On the 21st of March a proclamation was made telling the archbishops, bishops and other prelates, earls, barons, knights, citizens and burgesses in general that they might go home, but must be ready to appear again if the king summoned them. Those bishops, earls, barons, justices and others who were members of the council were to remain behind and so were all those who had still any business to transact. But the "parliament" was not at an end. Many of its doings that are recorded on our roll were done after the estates had been sent home. The king remained at Westminster, surrounded by his councillors, and his parliament was still in session as a "full" and "general" parliament as late as the 5th and 6th of April. Easter day fell on the 18th of that month, and its approach seems to have put an end to the prolonged session. Early in May the king began a tour through the home counties. He proposed to hold another "parliament," which however, so far as we know, was not to be an assembly of the estates, on the 15th of July, but this he postponed first to the 15th of August and then to the 15th of September.

Now if we are to frame any exact conception of the body or various bodies of men by whom the business that is recorded on our roll was transacted, and of the mode in which they dealt with that business, it seems necessary that we should understand the composition of the king's council. Unfortunately, as is well known, the council of Edward I. is still for us an ill-defined group of men. Writs of summons and writs for wages will often teach us the names of all the barons who were called to a parliament and enable us to know who it was that represented the pettiest boroughs, and yet we cannot enumerate with any certainty the members of the council. We can indeed make a list of those of its members who, not being prelates or barons, were summoned by name to be present at a given parliament. On the present occasion no less than thirty-three men were thus summoned. The list included Phillip Willoughby the chancellor of the exchequer, the justices of the two benches and the barons of the exchequer, several men who were being employed as justices in eyre and thirteen masters of the chancery or clerks of the council. The title "masters in chancery" is one which may lead us astray by suggesting that those who bear it are, like their successors in later days, principally engaged in performing certain subordinate functions in a great court of law and equity. But this is not so. If, with Dr. Stubbs, we say that at this time the chancellor is "the principal secretary of state for all departments," we may call these masters the "under-secretaries of state." Though already a keeper of the privy seal is beginning to intervene between the king and his chancellor, though already the king, at least at times, seems to have one yet more intimate clerk who is known as his secretary, the chancery is still the great secretarial department; it does nearly all the king's writing for him, whether such writing concerns foreign affairs or the government of England. If for a moment we may use such modern terms, we may say that the chancery is Home Office, Foreign Office, Board of Trade, Local Government Board all in one; in short it is a general secretarial bureau, which exercises a certain control even over the only other great official "department" that there is, namely the exchequer. Thus when the king is surrounded by the masters or principal clerks of the chancery, he has at his side the men who know most about the way in which England is governed and foreign affairs are managed, "permanent" or fairly permanent, "under-secretaries of state," and yet men who are on their promotion, for some of them may well look to being chancellors or treasurers before they die. It is among them also that the king finds his diplomatists. The thirty-three names therefore upon our list represent almost all that England has to show in the way of legal learning, official experience and administrative ability.

But then of course it is certain that there are members of the council who are not upon this list. They have been otherwise summoned. In the first place there are the two great ministers. The treasurer, Walter Langton, has been summoned as bishop of Lichfield; he is King Edward's right hand man. The chancellor, William Hamilton, who, when compared with Langton, seems an insignificant person, can appear as dean of York.[1] But there must be other prelates and there must be lay nobles who are members of the council. On the other hand it is difficult, if not impossible, to believe that every prelate or baron is a member of the council. We see this from that proclamation of the 21st of March which has already been mentioned. On that day the mass of prelates and nobles is sent home; but the members of the council are to remain behind. Now it would be a hard task were we to seek to recover the names of all those who in any given year were King Edward's sworn councillors. Still certain materials exist, by a circumspect use of which we might arrive at some tentative but serviceable conclusions. We will fix our attention on the months of March

[1] The chancellor seems to have had no summons, except as dean of York.

and April in the year 1305 and see by whom it is that the king is surrounded. Our parliament roll will give us some help, while some help may be derived from the contemporary charter roll. It is well known that a royal charter—and herein lies the chief formal difference between a charter and a mere patent—purports to have been delivered by the king in the presence of several witnesses whose names are given. We must not for one instant suggest that by merely collecting the names of such witnesses we could frame a list of those men of high station who were sworn members of the council. In the first place a man may be a member of the council and yet for many months together may never be in the king's presence. Sickness, old age, a mission to foreign parts, may keep him away; or again he may be in opposition or disgrace. No law obliges the king to consult all his councillors. For example, during the year in question we hardly ever see the Archbishop of Canterbury in the king's presence. In all likelihood he is still a member of the council; but he is in opposition and disgrace. And then on the other hand we may not infer that a man is a member of the council merely because he witnesses the grant of a charter. Not only may he be a casual visitor to the royal court, but even if his name appears habitually, this may be because he holds some not very important office about the king's person, and we can not be certain that the occupants of all such offices were usually sworn of the council.

Still we may reasonably ask what great men were constantly in the king's presence during these two months, and the answer that we get to this question may be of some value.

[There follow lists of those who witnessed the king's charters during the duration of this parliament.]

And now we may ask the question, what does our record tell us of the part played in this parliament by the king's council, and by those who constituted or represented the three estates of the realm? We may bring the business of a medieval parliament under five heads, namely—(1) the discussion of affairs of state, more especially foreign affairs; (2) legislation; (3) taxation or supply; (4) the audience of petitions; (5) judicial business, the determination of causes criminal and civil.

(1.) The king had summoned the estates in order that he might treat "of certain matters specially touching our realm of England and the establishment of our land of Scotland," and no doubt the state of Scotland was one of the main matters which required his attention and the advice of his councillors. Let us remember that just at this moment Edward was at the full height of his power. All looked well; it seemed as if the evening of his reign was to be peaceful and glorious. He had lately traversed Scotland from end to end hardly finding an enemy, save in the garrison of Stirling Castle, and now even Stirling was his. Wallace, it is true, was in all probability still at large when our parliament was sitting at Westminster; but he was a hunted outlaw and his capture, when it took place soon afterwards, cannot have been an unlooked-for event. As for the young Earl of Carrick, Edward had no reason for suspecting him of a grand ambition; we see him taking part in the parliament as one whom the king trusts. The task in hand was to provide for Scotland a settled form of government, a task that might demand prolonged debates, but not, it would seem, a hopeless task. What Edward did at this parliament was to call upon the Bishop of Glasgow, the Earl of Carrick, and John Mowbray to say how Scotland should be represented at another parliament to be holden later in the year. They reported that two bishops, two abbots, two earls, two barons, and two men elected by the community of Scotland would be representatives enough. As to the place at which the parliament should meet, they left that to the king; as to the time, the Scots could hardly be ready before Midsummer. Thereupon the king fixed London and the 15th of July as the place and date for the assembly. Afterwards he postponed that date until the 15th of September, and then at Westminster the ten Scottish representatives and twenty members of the English council drew up the important "Ordinatio super stabilitate terrae Scotiae." However, at the moment what should interest us most is this, that in our lenten parliament the three Scottish spokesmen did not answer the question that had been put to them until after the assembly of the English estates had been dissolved. Those who were not members of the council had been sent home on the 21st of March; not until the 26th did the Bishop of Glasgow, Robert Bruce, and John Mowbray bring in their report.

Whether Edward had sought advice in this matter from the mass of the clergy, baronage, and commoners, we cannot say; nor do we know that the affairs of Gascony afforded material for a general debate, though there was an enormous mass of Gascon business to be transacted. Edward had lately recovered his French provinces, and was just sending out a new set of representatives. John of Havering, who had been justiciar of Wales, was to be in supreme command as seneschal of the duchy; Richard of Havering, lately the escheator north of Trent, was to be constable of Bordeaux; William Dene, seneschal of the Agenais; Frisot de Montclar, treasurer of Agen. Vast quantities of writs had to be issued for the payment of arrears of many kinds.

To come nearer home, we have seen how the king expected that the clergy would make an attack upon him. He was now quite strong enough to meet, to forestall, such an attack. He had not forgotten the humiliation that he had suffered at the hands of Archbishop Winchelsea. With his very good will, as we may well suppose, a petition was presented by the barons and commons complaining that the monks, more especially the Cistercians, sent large sums of money out of the country to alien mother houses. Of this matter we must speak under another head, but it may have been discussed in many meetings by the assembled laity. The treatment of the offending archbishop, who had lately been giving a fresh cause of complaint by "visiting" the king's free chapel in Hastings Castle, was a subject to be debated rather at the council board than before the estates of the realm.

(2.) In the way of legislation this parliament did little. No statute was passed which at once found a place upon the statute roll; but there are several acts of a more or less legislative character. . . .

(3.) As to taxation, we have every reason to believe that on the present occasion no tax of any kind was imposed, and we have no evidence to show that the king asked for money.

(4.) . . . .

The petitions of which our roll speaks are neither petitions by parliament nor yet are they petitions addressed to parliament. We see at once that they are very different from those petitions of the commons (*petitions de la commune, petitions des communes*) which will occupy the greater part of almost any parliament roll of Edward III.'s day. But again they are not addressed to "parliament," or to "the lords of parliament," or to either house of parliament. They are addressed either "to the king" or "to the king and his council." In a certain sense they are parliamentary petitions, they are presented in or at a parliament. But at present "parliament" or "a parliament" is not conceived as a body that can be petitioned. A parliament is rather an act than a body of persons. One cannot present a petition to a colloquy, to a debate. It is but slowly that this word is appropriated to colloquies of a particular kind, namely, those which the king has with the estates of his realm, and still more slowly that it is transferred from the colloquy to the body of men whom the king has summoned. As yet any meeting of the king's council that has been solemnly summoned for general business seems to be a parliament.[2] These petitions are not addressed to parliament, nor are they addressed to the assembled estates, nor are they addressed to the earls, barons, and prelates. They are

[2] Stubbs, Const. Hist. § 230: "The name of parliament, the king's parliament, belonged to the sessions of each of the three bodies thus distinguished, the terminal session of the select council, the session of the great council, the session of the commune consilium of the three estates." Langlois, Revue Historique, xlii. 90: "Parlement ce mot vague, synonyme barbare, à l'origine, d'assemblée et de *colloquium*, s'est précisé vers la même époque en Angleterre et en France." The personification of "parliament," which enables us to say that laws are made by, and not merely in, parliament, is a slow and subtle process. The same process is now at work upon other words; we begin to personify the Church Congress and so forth; even our "meetings" pass resolutions. As to the word "council," it is important to remember that in the middle ages no distinction was or could be drawn between "council" and "counsel"; both were *consilium*.

addressed either simply to the king or to the king and his council. The formal title for them which is in use in the chancery is "petitiones de consilio," "council petitions."

When we examine the character of these petitions we soon see that for the more part they were not fit subjects for discussion in a large assembly. They do not ask for anything that could be called legislation; the responses that are given to them are in no sort "private acts of parliament." Generally the boon that is asked for is one which the king without transcending his legal powers might either grant or deny. Sometimes we may say that, if the facts are truly stated by the petitioner, the king is more or less strictly bound by the rules of common honesty to give him some relief:—The king owes him wages, or his lands have been wrongfully seized by the king's officers. At other times what is asked for is pure grace and favour:—The petitioner owes the king money and asks that he may be allowed to pay it by instalments, or that in consideration of his poverty part of his debt may be forgiven, or perhaps the University of Cambridge asks that the king will found a college. As yet no hard line is drawn between the true petition of right which shall be answered by a *Fiat justitia* and all other petitions. "Right" and "grace" shade off into each other by insensible degrees, and there is a wide field for governmental discretion. Probably there would be an outcry if the religious houses could not pretty easily obtain licenses for the acquisition of a reasonable quantity of land; if the nobleman who is going abroad were not suffered to appoint a general attorney; if the burghers of this or that town could not without much difficulty get leave to tax themselves and their neighbours by way of murage, pontage, or pavage; still in any particular case the request may be refused and no reason given for the refusal.

Further, we see that the response to the petition seldom gave to the suppliant all that he wanted. He had only, we may say, "made a *prima facie* case" for relief, and he obtained only a preliminary order. He did not get what he wanted, he was merely put in the way of getting it. Hale has stated this matter very well:—"But although the council received the petitions from the hands of the receivers, yet they rarely (if at all) exercised any decision or decisive jurisdiction upon them, but only a kind of deliberative power, or rather direction, transmitting them to the proper courts, places, or persons where they were proper to be decided. . . . Hence it is, that most of the answers that the council gave were in the nature of remissions of the petitions to those persons or courts that had properly the cognizance of the causes." That is so; but it does not imply that, had there been no petitions, those persons or courts would have been competent to entertain those causes or to have given relief to the aggrieved. These petitions and responses are not nugatory. Nothing in the age that we are studying is more remarkable than the narrowly limited powers of the courts of law, of the exchequer, of the chancery, more especially in all such matters as concern the king. The courts of law can in general only entertain such causes as are laid before them by a writ issued from the chancery. For ordinary cases the chancery has a store of "writs of course," and no doubt they are issued as a mere matter of routine upon receipt of the proper fees; but if anything that is in the least unusual is required, the chancellor will do nothing without a warrant from the king or council, and this warrant will be carefully noted at the foot of the writ. . . . The king has a very tight and immediate control not only over all purely governmental affairs, but also over all "administrative justice." This control is exercised for him in his "parliaments" by his council or by committees of his council, the greater cases and those which have most of "grace" in them being reserved for his own hearing. The exchequer, the financial department, is controlled by the chancery, the secretarial department, and the chancery is controlled by king and council. Often enough the man who wishes for relief in the exchequer must go first to the council for an endorsement and then to the chancery for a writ. There is already a great deal of what an impatient reader may call circumlocution and red tape. The petition will perhaps in the first instance be endorsed with a *Coram Rege*; it will then be taken before the king and another endorsement will be made upon it; a note of it will then be made upon the parliament roll; then it will be delivered into the chancery; from the chancery a writ will be sent to the exchequer but not until it has been copied on the close roll; when it gets to the exchequer, copies of it will be made by the remembrancers upon their memoranda rolls; and after all this the treasurer and barons will only begin to consider whether justice requires that the suppliant should have any relief. All this formalism is worthy of study; it is the necessary groundwork for ministerial responsibility and government by discussion.

The petitioner, we have said, had only "to make a *prima facie* case." Occasionally we find him sending in some evidence along with his petition, for example, a copy of a charter, or of an inquisition. This, however, is rare, and a petition hardly ever ends with a formal offer of proof such as that which every plaintiff makes in the courts of law. Still it seems plain that those who heard the petitions must have had before them more than the suppliant's bare and unsworn word about the facts of his case. True that they were seldom going to give him any final relief; usually they would do no more than set some inquiry going in the courts of law, the chancery or the exchequer. But then the institution of such inquiries cannot possibly have been a mere matter of course; had it been such, a clerk of the chancery might have been set to endorse the petitions with cut and dried formulas. The truth probably is that as regards the king's interests—and it is just because the king has some interest in the matter that most of these petitions are presented—the council is exceedingly well informed; potentially it is almost omniscient. In these parliaments the whole governmental force of England is brought into a focus. Not only are all the great officers there, but most of their principal subordinates are there or within call. A petitioner can hardly make a statement about the king's finances, the king's estates, or even the course of justice, that cannot at once be checked, if not by one of the auditors, then by some judge, clerk, remembrancer or escheator who is close at hand, or by a few recent rolls which are within easy reach. This, we take it, is what is meant by that "trying" of petitions of which we hear. The petitions reserved for the king himself are not to be placed before him until they have been sufficiently "tried," that is to say, he expects that when a petition is brought before him there will be some minister at hand to say whether there is any truth in the petitioner's allegations. We know that the work of hearing petitions was long and laborious; it had threatened to deprive the king and his chief advisers of any leisure for the great affairs of state; and we may well believe that the four hundred and fifty endorsements recorded by our roll represent the work of many hours.

Sometimes the petition comes from an individual, sometimes from a community. Of petitions presented by communities we have a considerable number. To say nothing of the religious houses and the two universities we have petitions by the communities of boroughs and by the communities of counties. And here we may perhaps see one of the duties of the knight who appears on behalf of a shire and of the representative burgess: he brings in and, it may be, urges by oral argument the petitions of that community which has sent him to the parliament. Then, again, we seem to have petitions which must have been drawn up during the parliament. Some instances we have already mentioned. "The bishops, abbots, earls, barons, and others of the realm" ask the king's aid in collecting their scutages. "The archbishops, bishops, prelates, earls, barons, and other good men of the land" ask that they may tallage such of the ancient demesnes of the crown as are in their hands. Such petitions seem to imply meetings at Westminster of those who were interested in them: they may imply regular sessions of the lords and the commons. By some resolution or another someone must have been authorised to write down these demands on strips of parchment. But so far as we can see these petitions are treated like the other petitions; on the parliament roll they are indiscriminately mixed up with the other petitions. We pass from a petition of the rector of Winchelsea, asking that the king will not take quite all the tithes of his church, to a petition presented by the magnates, and thence to a petition by the abbot of Osney concerning certain financial operations in which he has taken part on the king's behalf. Then again wedged between a petition of Roland of Okestead and a petition of the citizens of Lincoln we find two petitions which seem to come from the assembled commons and to be the outcome of their deliberations. "The poor men of England" complain that juries are corrupted by the rich, and that ecclesiastical judges meddle with temporal suits. In each case the king civilly refuses to do anything. If juries are corrupt, those who are injured can have a writ of attaint; a writ of prohibition will confine the courts christian within their proper bounds. By no sharp line can the petitions of the assembled lords and commoners be marked off from the general mass of those petitions which are to be "expedited" in the parliament by the king and his council. At a somewhat later date the line will be drawn; the petitions of the assembled commons, the petitions of "the community of the land," will be enrolled along with the king's answers to them; petitions addressed to either of the two houses will be enrolled, if they have received the assent of both houses and of the king; but the ordinary petitions presented to the king and council by those who have grievances will not be enrolled, though as of old many of them will be answered in parliament by committees of auditors.

As to what was done by the assembled commoners during the three weeks that they spent at Westminster, we shall hardly get beyond guesswork. All that we learn from our roll is, first, that they joined in a petition with the magnates about the exportation of the wealth of the monasteries, to which petition the king gave his consent, though he did not at once convert it into a statute; and secondly, that they presented two petitions of their own, which were refused. The king, so far as we know, did not ask them for money, nor did he desire their consent to any new law. The doctrine that in these days the representatives of the shires and towns were called to parliament not in order that they might act in concert on behalf of the commons of England, but in order that each might represent before the king in council the grievances and the interests of the particular community, county or borough, that sent him thither, may easily be pressed too far, but we shall probably think that there is no little truth in it, if we ask what the knights and burgesses were doing while the king and his councillors were slowly disposing of this great mass of petitions, many of which were presented by shires and boroughs. Official testimony the council can easily obtain; but it wants unofficial testimony also; it desires to know what men are saying in remote parts of England about the doings of sheriffs, escheators, and their like, and the possibilities of future taxation have to be considered. Then, again, there are many appointments to be made; for example, it is the fashion at this time to entrust a share in the work of delivering the county gaol to some knight of the county, very often to one of the knights who is representing or has represented that county at a parliament. Without denying that the germ of a "house" of commons already exists, without denying that its members hold meetings, discuss their common affairs and common grievances, without denying that Edward has encouraged them to do this—at the present moment he has a quarrel with the clergy, at least with the archbishop, and no doubt is glad when the assembled commons protest that there are abuses in the church—without denying all this, we may still believe that the council often gives audience, advice, instructions to particular knights and burgesses. After all we have to fall back upon the words of the writ of summons:—the commoners have been told to come in order that they may do what shall be ordained.

(5.) We pass to judicial business, noticing that the line between this and the hearing of petitions is not very sharp. The *Placita* which came before this parliament were few but miscellaneous.

In the first place we have the very famous case of Nicholas Segrave. Segrave and Cromwell had been serving with the king in his Scottish campaign; Segrave had brought an accusation against Cromwell and a judicial combat had been waged between them in the king's court. Then, however, Segrave, perhaps because he knew that the king would stop the duel, challenged his adversary to fight him in the court of the king of France; he withdrew himself from the English host and was endeavouring to make his way to France when he was captured. He confessed this grave offence—it was nothing less than treason. Edward then asked his council what was the punishment meet for such a crime. Their answer was—Death. The king, however, of his special grace was content that Segrave should find seven manucaptors who would undertake that he would render himself to prison if ever the king should call upon him to do so.

As regards the tribunal before which Segrave stood we can say this much:—The sheriff of Northampton was told to bring him before the king in the forthcoming parliament at Westminster, so soon as the king should arrive there:—He made his appearance "in full parliament in the presence of the king, the archbishop of Canterbury, and divers earls, barons and others of the king's council":—When sentence was to be pronounced the king asked the advice of "the earls, barons" (not, it will be observed, the prelates, for there was like to be a judgment of blood), "and others of his council":—It is said by a chronicler that they discussed the matter for three days:—Segrave's manucaptors appeared "before the king and his council" on the 29th of March and executed their bond on the 31st in the presence of the treasurer, three other bishops, the two chief justices, and others. The assembly of the estates had been dissolved on the 21st. It is very possible, however, that the trial took place while all the magnates were still at Westminster; Segrave was a baron and had been summoned as such to the parliament.

Such records as these—and many others of a like kind might be cited from other rolls—bring us within sight of an often debated and still debateable question. What in Edward I.'s day was the jurisdictional competence of the king's council, and in particular what was the relation in matters of judicature between the council and the nascent house of lords?

Perhaps some new light might fall upon this old question were we to view it from what might be called the archivist's standpoint, were we to say for the moment that every one of the high courts in England must have a separate set of rolls. If we take up this not indefensible position, and leave out of sight the chancery and the exchequer and also the courts of the itinerant justices, we shall then hold that Henry III. during the last half of his reign has two, and only two, high courts of law. The one of these is "the bench"; it has a separate set of records, "the *de banco* rolls." The other is professedly held before the king himself; it follows him in his movements; it has a separate set of records, "the *coram rege* rolls." For ordinary purposes this latter court consists of a few professional justices; later in the reign a chief justice is definitely appointed to hold the pleas *coram rege;* but at any moment this court can be afforced by the presence of the king, of his councillors, of numerous barons and prelates. Now and again its roll will bear as a title "Pleas before the King and his Council." It is superior to "the bench," for it can correct the errors of "the bench." Then early in Edward I.'s reign a further differentiation takes place. The court held *coram rege* when it assumes its everyday shape—that of a tribunal consisting of a few professional justices—becomes "the king's bench"; what has formerly been "the bench," though it always preserves this title, becomes, in common parlance, "the common bench"; at a later day it will be the court of common pleas. But there is a greater change than this. A new set, unfortunately a meagre, disjointed set, of plea rolls (which, however, are not pure plea rolls, for they deal also with petitions and other matters) begins to appear. A court which is to stand above the king's bench is being evolved out of the old court held *coram rege*; its rolls are the "parliament rolls." But the process is slow. For a while this highest tribunal is hardly distinct from the king's bench. Every plea in the king's bench is in theory a plea *coram ipso domino rege*, and the rolls of the king's bench never cease to be the *coram rege* rolls. The superior tribunal is rather, if we may so speak, an afforced, an intensified form of the inferior tribunal than a separate court; a plea that is put upon the parliament roll may be put upon the king's bench roll also; the justices of the king's bench are members of the council, and a case heard at a full meeting, a parliament, of the council, is heard by, among others, the justices of the king's bench. A plea may be adjourned from a parliament to the king's bench or from the king's bench to a parliament without breach of continuity.

A new tribunal is evolved, or rather, two tribunals become three. We can see this development taking place in the pages of Bracton and Fleta. Bracton knows but two of those courts of which we are speaking: there are justices resident at the bench; there are yet more exalted justices attending the king's person. Fleta knows three: there are justices resident at the bench; there are other justices who fill the king's own place, but above even them there is another tribunal, "for the king has his court in his council in his parliaments, in the presence of prelates, earls, barons, nobles, and other learned men, where judicial doubts are determined, and new remedies are established for new wrongs, and justice is done to every one according to his deserts." Bracton has to account for two sets of rolls; Fleta for three. Whether we ought to say that the highest of the three tribunals is the new one, whether we ought to describe the process as the deposit of a middle tribunal between the lowest and the highest, whether both of these phrases are not too definite and too modern to describe the real facts—these are grave problems which must be left to others. Our imaginary archivist would perhaps say that he could not decide them until he had made up his mind on the humbler question whether many parliament rolls have been lost. Our present point must be that before the end of Edward's reign there are three courts each with its roll.

What is the nature of the highest of these three?

Is it council, is it house of lords? Fleta will warn us that we are asking an almost unanswerable question. "Habet enim Rex curiam suam in consilio suo in parliamentis suis, praesentibus praelatis, comitibus, baronibus, proceribus et aliis viris peritis," that is all that we can safely say. The highest tribunal of the realm is the king in council; it is the king in his council in his parliaments, in the presence of prelates, barons, and other learned men. To deny that it is the king in council is impossible; to deny that it is the king in parliament, or rather that its sessions are parliaments, is impossible.

Events which were still in the future when the great Edward died, decided that the highest ordinary tribunal of the realm should be "the king in parliament," and that this term should mean the house of lords; they decided that this tribunal should become for the more part but a court of error, and during the rest of the middle ages and far into modern times should have exceedingly little to do; they decided also that the king in council should dispense an extraordinary justice and this on a very large scale. If asked to mark the difference between ordinary and extraordinary justice, we can hardly do better at the present moment than place ourselves once more in the archivist's room, and say that the court of ordinary jurisdiction keeps a proper Latin plea roll and that the council keeps none. This is no insignificant detail. When the time has come for abolishing that court of star chamber which is one of the forms that the council has assumed, this will be charged against it as one of its many irregularities—it has no proper Latin plea roll. In the eyes of the lawyers of the seventeenth century this want of a roll goes far to prove that the council board is an upstart tribunal. What has been its strength in time gone by when, having no stiff Latin record to draw up, it could modify its procedure to suit every new want, has become its weakness in the age of Coke and Prynne, an age which demands a parchment title for every unpopular institution.

Long ago the parliament roll has passed from the custody of the council. Long ago it has become the record of those meetings of the estates of the realm which have acquired an exclusive right to the name of parliaments, and more particularly it has become the record of the house of lords. Long ago, the rule has been that those members of the council who are not peers of the realm, but yet are summoned to parliament, are to sit in the house of lords as "mere assistants," are not to vote, are not to speak unless their opinions are demanded. This being so, we are apt to approach the parliament rolls of Edward I.'s reign with a certain prejudice in our minds. They ought, so we think, to be the records of the estates of the realm; in so far as they are judicial records, they ought to be the records of the house of lords. It is hard to think away out of our heads a history which has long lain in a remote past but which once lay in the future; it is hard to be ever remembering that such ancient terms as *house of lords* and *peers of the realm* were once new terms; it is hard to look at the thirteenth century save by looking at it through the distorting medium of the fourteenth. And so we are apt to approach our earliest parliament rolls with a belief that they ought to be rolls of the house of lords and not rolls of the king's council, that the supreme tribunal of England ought to be the house of lords and not the king's council, that, whatever upon our record makes against this belief should be explained away as irregular or anomalous.

Even if he had settled opinions about debateable questions of constitutional history, it would be wrong for the editor of such a book as this to thrust them forward. The most that he can legitimately do is to provide materials for the formation of opinions. In so doing, however, it may perhaps be lawful and desirable that he should remind his readers of some facts that are like to be forgotten. And in the present case he may be allowed to say once more that we have very few parliament rolls of Edward I.'s reign, to remark that his son's reign was filled with momentous events, and to plead that those events may not be suffered to cast their shadow over the past. We must judge the rolls of Edward I.'s reign on their own merits without reference to the parliament rolls of his grandson's, or of any later, reign. As regards the matter that is now before us, the jurisdictional competence of the parliaments, there seem to be some special reasons why this warning should not be neglected.

We are dealing with something that is new. However ancient may be the roots whence the jurisdiction of "the king in his council in his parliaments" draws its nourishment, it is a new thing that men should see three different tribunals rising one above the other; it is a new thing that they should see a yet higher court above that court which is held in theory *coram ipso domino Rege*. The competence of this highest court is as yet indefinite. Fleta uses vague words about it. He has a fairly clear view of the competence of the king's bench; it hears criminal causes; it corrects the errors and false judgments of all justices, except when such matters are brought before the king himself and his council or before auditors specially assigned for the purpose. But of the justice that is done by the king "in his council in his parliaments," we must speak loosely:—Judicial doubts are there decided, new remedies are provided for new wrongs, and justice is done to every one according to his merits. We can see, however, that this tribunal is not solely a court of error; it has a far wider power than the house of lords will have in later days. This doctrine is fully borne out by the parliament rolls. The causes which come before the parliaments do not usually come there by writ of error. The jurisdiction that is exercised is more commonly than not a jurisdiction of first instance. If we ask why a case comes before a parliament rather than before the king's bench or the common bench, often we can give no certain answer. We may say perhaps—to take examples from our own roll—that Nicholas Segrave is tried in a parliament because he is a baron charged with treason; but why should the citizens of Winchester be haled before a parliament for suffering a prisoner to escape, and why should not the Bishop of Salisbury urge his claim to tallage the men of Salisbury before one of the two benches, or even before the exchequer? Seemingly all that we dare say is that the causes heard in parliament are important causes, important because they concern the king, or because they concern very great men, or because they involve grave questions of public law, or because they are unprecedented. We must not miss the "equitableness" of this tribunal. When Fleta says that it provides new remedies for new wrongs, and that justice is done to every man according to his deserts, he means that this supreme court can look at "the merits of the case" with some disregard for technicalities. We are dealing with a court that has large, indefinite powers.

And then we are dealing with Edward I., the wise and vigorous king. Under his hand institutions which to our eyes seem to have in them many flaws, flaws which may easily become yawning clefts, are doing their appointed work without much friction. We can hardly look back to his time through the fourteenth century without imagining that there must be some jealous dislike of the council, an aristocratic jealousy on the part of the nobles, a professional jealousy on the part of the judges and common lawyers. But do we really see this? If not, then our problem as to the constitution of the supreme tribunal becomes simpler. It may be further simplified if we try to make it a concrete problem. Indubitably this supreme tribunal is the council. The question whether it is also the house of lords may be divided into two. First, we ought to ask whether every prelate and baron had a right to sit in the council though he had not been invited to do so. Secondly, we ought to ask whether those members of the council who were neither prelates nor barons were fully competent members of the tribunal.

To neither of these questions must we here give a dogmatic answer, but in connexion with the first it may be right that we should ask a yet further question, namely, whether we are not introducing an inappropriate idea and burdening ourselves with an unnecessary anachronism when we talk of any man having a right to sit in this or any other court of law? We must put duty in the first line, right in the second. We have learnt to do this when discussing the constitution of those county courts which send knights to the house of commons; must we not also do it when we are discussing the constitution of the house of lords and of the council? In 1305 the baron, who had come from Yorkshire or Devonshire, had been compelled to spend three weeks in London at his own cost, for he was paid no wages. Did he very much want to spend another three weeks there hearing dreary petitions concerning the woes of Scots and Gascons? At a later time a desire for political power and for social preeminence will make the English baron eager to insist on his right to a writ of summons, eager to take a part, however subordinate, in all that is done by the house of lords. But in Edward I.'s day the baronage is hardly as yet a well-defined body, and it may be that there are many men who, unable to foresee that their "blood" is being "ennobled" for ever and ever, are not best pleased when they receive a writ which tells them that, leaving their homes and affairs, they must journey and labour in the king's service, and all this at their own cost. Thus for many years one great constitutional question can remain in suspense. It is not raised, no one wishes to raise it. So long as the king does not impose taxes or issue statutes without the consent of the baronage, the baron hopes that the king will mind his own business (and it is his business to govern the realm) and allow other folk to mind theirs.

Of the second of our two questions but one word can here be said. If we fix our gaze on the council which remains in constant session and "in full parliament" at Westminster for several weeks after the generality of prelates and barons have departed, we shall have some difficulty in believing that those councillors who are neither prelates nor barons are taking but a subordinate part in the work that is done; for example, that when the council is sitting as a judicial tribunal, the opinions of the two chief justices, Brabazon and Hengham, are of less importance than the opinions of two barons who are no lawyers. Once more let us remember that until very lately the jurisdiction of the king's council has been regarded as being substantially the same thing as the jurisdiction of that court over which Brabazon presides.

II

The Meanings of Words

Pollock and Maitland's History of English Law before the Time of Edward I *was published in 1895 in two volumes and quickly became and has remained the standard general authority on English legal history down to the thirteenth century. A second edition appeared in 1898. In 1897, a year before the second edition of the* History *appeared, Maitland's* Domesday Book and Beyond *was published. The greater part of this "classic" had been written for inclusion in the* History, *but a change of plan caused its omission. Extracts from the* History *are given on pages 81-93 and those on pages 94-105 are from* Domesday Book and Beyond.

The Unfree

In the main, then, all free men are equal before the law. Just because this is so the line between the free and the unfree seems very sharp. And the line between freedom and unfreedom is the line between freedom and servitude. Bracton accepts to the full the

Roman dilemma: *Omnes homines aut liberi sunt aut servi.* He will have no mere unfreedom, no semi-servile class, no merely praedial serfage, nothing equivalent to the Roman *colonatus.* All men are either free men or serfs, and every serf is as much a serf as any other serf. We use the word *serf,* not the word *slave;* but it is to be remembered that Bracton had not got the word *slave.* He used the worst word that he had got, the word which, as he well knew, had described the Roman slave whom his owner might kill. And the serf has a *dominus;* we may prefer to render this by *lord* and not by *master* or *owner,* and it is worthy of observation that medieval Latin can not express this distinction; if the serf has a *dominus,* the palatine earl, nay, the king of England, so long as he is duke of Aquitaine, has a *dominus* also, and this is somewhat in the serf's favour; but still Bracton uses the only words by which he could have described a slave and a slave-owner. True that *servus* is neither the commonest nor yet the most technical name for the unfree man; more commonly he is called *villanus* or *nativus,* and these are the words used in legal pleadings; but for Bracton these three terms are interchangeable, and though efforts, not very consistent or successful efforts, might be made to distinguish between them, and some thought it wrong to call the villeins serfs, still it is certain that *nativus* always implied personal unfreedom, that *villanus* did the same when employed by lawyers, and that

Bracton was right in saying that the law of his time knew no degrees of personal unfreedom. Even in common practice and by men who were not jurists the word *servus* was sometimes used as an equivalent for *nativus* or *villanus*. The jurors of one hundred will call all the unfree people *servi*, while in the next hundred they will be *villani*. In French *villein* is the common word; but the feminine of *villein* is *nieve* (*nativa*).

There are no degrees of personal unfreedom; there is no such thing as merely praedial serfage. A free man may hold in villeinage; but that is an utterly different thing; he is in no sort a serf; so far from being bound to the soil he can fling up his tenement and go whithersoever he pleases. In later centuries certain niceties of pleading gave rise to the terms "villein in gross" and "villein regardant," and in yet later times, when villeinage of any kind was obsolescent, these were supposed to point to two different classes of men, the villein regardant being inseverable from a particular manor, while the villein in gross might be detached from the soil and sold as a chattel. The law of Bracton's time recognizes no such distinction. As a matter of fact and a matter of custom, English serfage may well be called praedial. In the first place, it rarely if ever happens that the serfs are employed in other work than agriculture and its attendant processes; their function is to cultivate their lord's demesne. In the second place, the serf usually holds more or less land, at least a cottage, or else is the member of a household whose head holds land, and the services that he does to his lord are constantly regarded in practice as the return which is due from him in respect of this tenement or even as the return due from the tenement itself; such services, as we have already seen, are often minutely defined by custom. In the third place, his lord does not feed or clothe him; he makes his own living by cultivating his villein tenement, or, in case he is but a cottager, by earning wages at the hand of his wealthier neighbours. In the fourth place, he is seldom severed from his tenement; he is seldom sold as a chattel, though this happens now and again; he passes from feoffor to feoffee, from ancestor to heir as annexed to the soil. For all this, the law as administered by the king's court permits his lord to remove him from the tenement. It could hardly have done otherwise, for he held in villeinage, and even a free man holding in villeinage could be ejected from his tenement whenever the lord pleased without finding a remedy before the king's justices. But as to the serf, not only could he be removed from one tenement, he could be placed in another; his lord might set him to work of any kind; the king's court would not interfere; for he was a *servus* and his person belonged to his lord; "he was merely the chattel of his lord to give and sell at his pleasure."

But, whatever terms the lawyers may use, their own first principles will forbid us to speak of the

English "serf" as a slave: their own first principles, we say, for what we find is not a general law of slavery humanely mitigated in some details, but a conception of serfdom which at many points comes into conflict with our notion of slavery. In his treatment of the subject Bracton frequently insists on the relativity of serfdom. Serfdom with him is hardly a status; it is but a relation between two persons, serf and lord. As regards his lord the serf has, at least as a rule, no rights; but as regards other persons he has all or nearly all the rights of a free man; it is nothing to them that he is a serf. Now this relative serfdom we cannot call slavery. As regards mankind at large the serf so far from being a mere thing is a free man. This seems to be the main principle of the law of Bracton's day. We must now examine each of its two sides: the serf's rightlessness as regards his lord, his freedom or "quasi-freedom" as regards men in general. It will then remain to speak of his relation to the state.

Such briefly stated is the English law of villeinage or serfage in the thirteenth century. Its central idea, that of the relativity of serfage, is strange. It looks artificial: that is to say, it seems to betray the handiwork of lawyers who have forced ancient facts into a modern theory. Slavery is very intelligible; so is slavery tempered by humane rules which will forbid an owner to maltreat his human chattel; so again is a praedial serfage, and the ancient laws of our race compel us to admit that there may be a half-free class, men who are neither *liberi homines* nor yet *servi;* but a merely relative serfdom is a juristic curiosity. In defining it we have ever to be using the phrases "in relation to," "as regards," "as against," phrases which would not easily occur to the unlettered, and law which allows my serf to sue any free man but me, even to sue my lord, does not look like a natural expression of any of those deep-seated sentiments which demand that divers classes of men shall be kept asunder. Then this idea of relative servitude has to be further qualified before it will square with facts and customs and current notions of right and wrong. When a lord allows it to be recorded that on the death of his servile tenant he is entitled to the best beast, he goes very far towards admitting that he is not entitled to seize the chattels of his serf without good cause. We hesitate before we describe the serf as rightless even as against his lord, and, if we infer want of right from want of remedy, we feel that we may be doing violence to the thoughts of a generation which saw little difference between law and custom. On the whole looking at the law of Bracton's day we might guess that here as elsewhere the king's court has been carrying out a great work of simplification; we might even guess that its "serf-villein," rightless against his lord, free against all but his lord, is as a matter of history a composite person, a serf and a villein rolled into one.

Seisin

In the history of our law there is no idea more cardinal than that of seisin. Even in the law of the present day it plays a part which must be studied by every lawyer; but in the past it was so important that we may almost say that the whole system of our land law was law about seisin and its consequences.

Seisin is possession. A few, but only a few words about etymology may be ventured. The inference has been too hastily drawn that this word speaks to us of a time of violence, when he who seized land was seised of it, when seizing land was the normal mode of acquiring possession. Now doubtless there is an etymological connexion between "seizing" and being "seised," but the nature of that connexion is not very certain. If on the one hand "seisin" is connected with "to seize," on the other hand it is connected with "to sit" and "to set":—the man who is seised is the man who is sitting on land; when he was put in seisin he was set there and made to sit there. Thus seisin seems to have the same root as the German *Besitz* and the Latin *possessio*. To our medieval lawyers the word *seisina* suggested the very opposite of violence; it suggested peace and quiet. It did so to Coke. "And so it was said as *possessio* is derived *a pos et sedeo*, because he who is in possession may sit down in rest and quiet; so *seisina* also is derived *a sedendo*, for till he hath seisin all is *labor et dolor et vexatio spiritus*; but when he has obtained seisin, he may *sedere et acquiescere*."

The would-be Latin words *seisina, seisire,* came in with the Conqueror; but in all probability they did but translate cognate English terms. When in a famous passage the Saxon Chronicle tells us that "ealle tha landsittende men" swore fealty to William, it tells what was done by all who were seised of land. "To sit upon land" had been a common phrase, meaning to possess land; in the cartularies we read of *landseti, cotseti, ferlingseti, undersetles,* as of various classes of tenants. To this day we call the person who takes possession of land without having title to it a "mere squatter"; we speak of "the sitting tenant," and such a phrase as "a country seat" puts us at the right point of view. The seated man is in quiet enjoyment. We reverence the throne, the bishop's see, "the Right Reverend Bench," the bench of judges, we obey the orders of the chair; the powers that be are seated.

Now in course of time *seisin* becomes a highly technical word; but we must not think of it having been so always. Few, if any, of the terms in our legal vocabulary have always been technical terms. The licence that the man of science can allow himself of coining new words is one which by the nature of the case is denied to lawyers. They have to take their terms out of the popular speech; gradually the words so taken are defined; sometimes a word continues to have both a technical meaning for lawyers and a different and vaguer meaning for laymen; sometimes the word that lawyers have adopted is abandoned by the laity. Such for a long time past has been the fate of *seisin*.

When we say that seisin is possession, we use the latter term in the sense in which lawyers use it, a sense in which possession is quite distinct from, and may be sharply opposed to, proprietary right. In common talk we constantly speak as though possession were much the same as ownership. When a man says "I possess a watch," he generally means "I own a watch." Suppose that he has left his watch with a watchmaker for repair, and is asked whether he still possesses a watch, whether the watch is not in the watchmaker's possession, and if so whether both he and the watchmaker have possession of the same watch at the time time, he is perhaps a little puzzled and resents our questions as lawyers' impertinences. Even if the watch has been stolen, he is not very willing to admit that he no longer possesses a watch. This is instructive:—in our non-professional moments *possession* seems much nearer to our lips than *ownership*. Often however we slur over the gulf by means of the conveniently ambiguous verbs "have" and "have got"—I have a watch, the watchmaker has it—I have a watch, but some one else has got it. But so soon as there is any law worthy of the name, right and possession must emerge and be contrasted:—so soon as any one has said "You have got what belongs to me," the germs of these two notions have appeared and can be opposed to each other. Bracton is never tired of emphasizing the contrast. In so doing he constantly makes use of the Roman terms, *possessio* on the one hand, *proprietas* or *dominium* on the other. These are not the technical terms of English law; but it has terms which answer a like purpose, *seisina* on the one hand, *ius* on the other. The person who has right may not be seised, the person who is seised may not be seised of right.

The idea of seisin seems to be closely connected in our ancestors' minds with the idea of enjoyment. A man is in seisin of land when he is enjoying it or in a position to enjoy it; he is seised of an advowson (for of "incorporeal things" there may be seisin) when he presents a parson who is admitted to the church; he is seised of freedom from toll when he successfully resists a demand for payment. This connexion is brought out by the interesting word *esplees* (*expleta*). In a proprietary action for land the demandant will assert that he, or some ancestor of his, was "seised of the land in his demesne as of fee and of right, by taking thence esplees to the value of five shillings, as in corn and other issues of the land." The man who takes and enjoys the fruits of the earth thereby "exploits" his seisin, that is to say, he makes his seisin "explicit," visible to the eyes of his neighbours. In order that a seisin may have all its legal effects it must be thus exploited. Still a man must have seisin before he can exploit it, and therefore in a possessory action it is unnecessary for the plaintiff to allege this taking of esplees. The moment at which he acquires his seisin may not be the right moment for mowing hay or reaping corn. Seisin of land therefore is not the enjoyment of the fruits of the earth; it is rather that state of things which in due time will render such an enjoyment possible.

Law must define this vague idea, and it can not find the whole essence of possession in visible facts. It is so now-a-days. We see a man in the street carrying an umbrella; we can not at once tell whether or no he possesses it. Is he its owner, is he a thief, is he a borrower, a hirer, is he the owner's servant? If he is the owner, he possesses it; if he is a thief, he possesses it. If he is the owner's servant, we shall probably deny his possession. If he is a borrower, we may have our doubts; the language of every-day life may hesitate about the matter; law must make up its mind. Before we attribute possession to a man, we must apparently know something about the intentions that he has in regard to the thing, or rather about the intentions that he must be supposed to have when the manner in which he came by the thing has been taken into consideration. Probably the better way of stating the matter is not to speak of his real intentions, which are often beside the mark, nor of the intentions that he must be supposed to have, which are fictions, but to say at once that we require to know how he came by the thing. This being known, problems await us. If the carrier of the umbrella is its owner, he possesses it; if he is a thief making off with a stolen chattel, he possesses it; if he has by mistake taken what he believes to be his own, he probably possesses it; if he has borrowed it or hired it, the case is not so plain; law must decide—and various systems of law will decide differently—whether possession shall be attributed to the borrower or to the lender, to the letter or the hirer.

When deciding to whom it would attribute a seisin, our medieval law had to contemplate a complex mass of facts and rights. In the first place, the actual occupant of the soil, who was cultivating it and taking its fruits, might be so doing in exercise, or professed exercise, of any one of many different rights. He might be there as tenant at will, tenant for term of years, tenant in villeinage, tenant for life, tenant in dower, tenant by the curtesy, tenant in fee simple, guardian of an infant, and so forth. But further, at the same moment many persons might have and be actually enjoying rights of a proprietary kind in the same plot of ground. Giles would be holding in villeinage of Ralph, who held in free socage of the abbot, who held in frankalmoin of the earl, who held by knight's service of the king. There would be the case of the reversioner to be considered and the case of the remainderman.

In the thirteenth century certain lines have been firmly drawn. The royal remedies for the protection of seisin given by Henry II. were given only to those who were seised "of a free tenement": the novel disseisin lies when a man has been disseised *de libero tenemento suo*. Doubtless these words were intended to exclude those who held in villeinage. This is well brought out by a change in the language of Magna Carta. The original charter of 1215 by its most famous clause declares that no free man is to be disseised, unless it be by the lawful judgment of his peers or the law of the land. The charter of 1217 inserts the words "de libero tenemento suo vel libertatibus vel liberis consuetudinibus suis." It is not intended, it would not be suffered, that a man holding in villeinage, even though personally *liber homo*, should have a possession protected by the king's court. Such a tenant is not seised of free tenement, and, as royal justice is now beginning to supplant all other justice, it is said that he has no seisin recognized by the common law. The lord of whom he holds is the person protected by the common law, and is seised *de libero tenemento*; if you eject the villein tenant, you disseise the lord. But within the sphere of manorial justice this tenant is seised—seisin has been delivered to him by the rod according to the custom of the manor—and when he pleads in the manorial court he will say that he is seised according to the custom of the manor. Here then already we have a dual seisin:—the lord seised *quoad* the king's courts and the common law, the tenant seised *quoad* the lord's court and the manorial custom.

Then again, we ought not to look to Domesday Book for a settled and stable scheme of technical terms. Such a scheme could not be established in a brief twenty years. About one half of the technical terms that meet us, about one half of the terms which, as we think, ought to be precisely defined, are, we may say, English terms. They are ancient English words, or they are words brought hither by the Danes, or they are Latin words which have long been in use in England and have acquired special meanings in relation to English affairs. On the other hand, about half the technical terms are French. Some of them are old Latin words which have acquired special meanings in France, some are Romance words newly coined in France, some are Teutonic words which tell of the Frankish conquest of Gaul. In the one great class we place *scira, hundredum, wapentac, hida, berewica, inland, haga, soka, saka, geldum, gablum, scotum, heregeat, gersuma, thegnus, sochemannus, burus, coscet;* in the other *comitatus, carucata, virgata, bovata, arpentum, manerium, feudum, alodium, homagium relevium, baro, vicecomes, vavassor, villanus, bordarius, colibertus, hospes.* It is not in twenty years that a settled and stable scheme can be formed out of such elements as these. And often enough it is very difficult for us to give just the right meaning to some simple

Latin word. If we translate *miles* by *soldier* or *warrior*, this may be too indefinite; if we translate it by *knight*, this may be too definite, and yet leave open the question whether we are comparing the *miles* of 1086 with the *cniht* of unconquered England or with the knight of the thirteenth century. If we render *vicecomes* by *sheriff* we are making our sheriff too little of a *vicomte*. When *comes* is before us we have to choose between giving Britanny an *earl*, giving Chester a *count*, or offending some of our *comites* by invidious distinctions. Time will show what these words shall mean. Some will perish in the struggle for existence; others have long and adventurous careers before them. At present two sets of terms are rudely intermixed; the time when they will grow into an organic whole is but beginning.

To this we must add that, unless we have mistaken the general drift of legal history, the law implied in Domesday Book ought to be for us very difficult law, far more difficult than the law of the thirteenth century, for the thirteenth century is nearer to us than is the eleventh. The grown man will find it easier to think the thoughts of the schoolboy than to think the thoughts of the baby. And yet the doctrine that our remote forefathers being simple folk had simple law dies hard. Too often we allow ourselves to suppose that, could we but get back to the beginning, we should find that all was intelligible and should then be able to watch the process whereby simple ideas were smothered under subtleties and technicalities. But it is not so. Simplicity is the outcome of technical subtlety; it is the goal not the starting point. As we go backwards the familiar outlines become blurred; the ideas become fluid, and instead of the simple we find the indefinite.

Of the legal position of the *servus* Domesday Book tells us little or nothing; but earlier and later documents oblige us to think of him as a slave, one who in the main has no legal rights. He is the *theów* of the Anglo-Saxon dooms, the *servus* of the ecclesiastical canons. But though we do right in calling him a slave, still we might well be mistaken were we to think of the line which divides him from other men as being as sharp as the line which a mature jurisprudence will draw between thing and person. We may well doubt whether this principle—"The slave is a thing, not a person"—can be fully understood by a grossly barbarous age. It implies the idea of a person, and in the world of sense we find not persons but men.

Thus degrees of servility are possible. A class may stand, as it were, half-way between the class of slaves and the class of free men. The Kentish law of the seventh century as it appears in the dooms of Aethelbert, like many of its continental sisters, knows a class of men who perhaps are not free men and yet are not slaves; it knows the *laet* as well as the *theów*. From what race the Kentish *laet* has sprung, and how, when it comes to details, the law will treat him—these are obscure questions, and the latter of them can not be answered unless we apply to him what is written about the *laeti*, *liti* and *lidi* of the continent. He is thus far a person that he has a small wergild but possibly he is bound to the soil. Only in Aethelbert's dooms do we read of him. From later days, until Domesday Book breaks the silence, we do not obtain any definite evidence of the existence of any class of men who are not slaves but none the less are tied to the land. Of men who are bound to do heavy labour services for their lords we do hear, but we do not hear that if they run away they can be captured and brought back. As we shall see by and by, Domesday Book bears witness to the existence of a class of *buri*, *burs*, *coliberti*, who seem to be distinctly superior to the *servi*, but distinctly inferior to the villeins, bordiers and cottiers. It is by no means impossible that they, without being slaves, are in a very proper and intelligible sense unfree men, that they have civil rights which they can assert in courts of law, but that they are tied to the soil. The gulf between the seventh and the eleventh centuries is too wide to allow of our connecting them with the *laet* of Aethelbert's laws, but still our documents are not exhaustive enough to justify us in denying that all along there has been a class (though it can hardly have been a large class) of men who could not quit their tenements and yet were no slaves. As we shall see hereafter, liberty was in certain contexts reckoned a matter of degree; even the *villanus*, even the *sochemannus* was not for every purpose *liber homo*. When this is so, the *theów* or *servus* is like to appear as the unfreest of persons rather than as no person but a thing.

In truth the vast class of men that we are examining must have been heterogeneous to a high degree. Not only were some members of it much wealthier than others, but in all probability some were economically subject to others. So it was in later days. In the thirteenth century we may easily find a manor in which the lord is paying hardly any wages. He gets nearly all his agricultural work done for him by his villeins and his cottiers. Out of his cottiers however he will get but one day's work in the week. If then we ask what the cottiers are doing during the rest of their time, the answer surely must be that they are often working as hired labourers on the villein's virgates, for a cottier can not have spent five days in the week over the tillage of his poor little tenement. It is a remarkable feature of the manorial arrangement that the meanest of the lord's *nativi* are but rarely working for him. Thus if we were to remove the lord in order that the village community might be revealed, we should still see not only rich and poor, but employers and employed, villagers and "undersettles."

Now all these people are in a sense unfree, while yet in some other sense they are free. Let us spend a short while in discussing the various meanings that freedom may have in a legal classification of the sorts and conditions of men. When we have put out of account the rightless slave, who is a thing, it still remains possible to say that some men are unfree, while others are free, and even that freedom is a matter of degree. But we may use various standards for the measurement of liberty.

Perhaps in the first place we shall think of what German writers call *Freizügigkeit*, the power to leave the master whom one has been serving. This power our ancestors would perhaps have called "fare-worthiness." If the master has the right to recapture the servant who leaves his service, or even if he has the right to call upon the officers of the state to pursue him and bring him back to his work, then we may account this servant an unfree man, albeit the relation between him and his master has been created by free contract. Such unfreedom is very distinct from rightlessness. As a freak of jurisprudence we might imagine a modern nobleman entitled to reduce by force and arms his fugitive butler to well-paid and easy duties, while all the same that butler had rights against all the world including his master, had access to all courts, and could even sue for his wages if they were not punctually paid. If we call him unfree, then freedom will look like a matter of degree, for the master's power to get back his fugitive may be defined by law in divers manners. May he go in pursuit and use force? Must he send a constable or sheriff's officer? Must he first go to court and obtain a judgment, "a decree for specific performance" of the contract of service? The right of recapture seems to shade off gradually into a right to insist that a breach of the contract of service is a criminal offence to be punished by fine or imprisonment.

Then, again, there may seem to us to be more of unfreedom in the case of one who was born a servant than in the case of one who has contracted to serve, though we should note that one may be born to serve without being born rightless.

More to the point than these obvious reflections will be the remark that in the thirteenth century we learn to think of various spheres or planes of justice. A right good in one sphere may have no existence in another. The rights of the villeins in their tenements are sanctioned by manorial justice; they are ignored by the king's courts. Here, again, the ideas of freedom and unfreedom find a part to play. True that in the order of legal logic freedom may precede royal protection; a tenure is protected because it is free; still men are soon arguing that it is free because it is protected, and this probably discloses an idea which lies deep:—the king's courts, the national courts, are open to the free; we approach the rightlessness of the slave if our rights are recognized only in a court of which our lord is the president.

The thirteenth century will also supply us with the notion that continuous agricultural service, service in which there is a considerable element of uncertainty, is unfree service. Where from day to day the lord's will counts for much in determining the work that his tenants must do, such tenants, even if they be free men, are not holding freely. But uncertainty is a matter of degree, and therefore unfreedom may easily be regarded as a matter of degree.

Then, again, in the law books of the Norman age we see distinct traces of a usage which would make *liber* or *liberalis* an equivalent for our *noble*, or at least for our *gentle*. The common man with the wergild of 200 shillings, though indubitably he is no *servus*, is not *liberalis homo*.

Lastly, in our thirteenth century we learn that privileges and exceptional immunities are "liberties" and "franchises." What is our definition of a liberty, a franchise? A portion of royal power in the hands of a subject. In Henry III.'s day we do not say that the Earl of Chester is a freer man, more of a *liber homo*, than is the Earl of Gloucester, but we do say that he has more, greater, higher liberties.

Therefore we shall not be surprised if in Domesday Book what we read of freedom, of free men, of free land is sadly obscure. Let us then observe that the *villanus* both is and is not a free man.

It has sometimes been said that a feudal tenure was the only kind of land tenure that the Norman conquerors could conceive. In a certain sense this may be true, but we should have preferred to say that probably they could not easily conceive a kind of tenure that was not dependent:—every one who holds land (except he be the king) holds it of someone else. The adjective "feudal" was not in their vocabulary, and their use of the word *feudum*—occasionally we meet the older *feum*—is exceedingly obscure. Very rarely does it denote a tenure or a mass of rights; usually, though it may connote rights of a certain order, it denotes a stretch of land; thus we may read of the fee of the Bishop of Bayeux, thereby being meant the territory which the bishop holds. Occasionally, however, we hear of a man holding land *in feudo*. One instance may be enough to show that such a phrase did not imply military tenure:—"William the Chamberlain held this manor *in feudo* of the Queen [Matilda] at a rent of £3 a year and after her death he held it in the same fashion of the king." All sense of militariness, and all sense of precariousness, that the word has ever had in its continental history, seems to be disappearing. Already the process has begun which will make it applicable to every person who has heritable rights in land. William the Chamberlain is, we take it, already a fee farmer, that is, a rent-paying tenant with heritable rights. As to the word *beneficium*, which *feum* or *feudum* has been supplanting, we shall hardly find it with its old meaning. It seems to be holding its own only within the sphere of ecclesiastical rights, where the "benefice" will survive until our own day.

A yet more interesting and equally foreign word is not unfrequently used, namely, *alodium*. The Norman commissioners deemed that a large number of

English tenants in Kent, Sussex, Surrey and Hampshire and some in Berkshire had been *alodiarii* or *aloarii* and had held *in alodium* or *sicut alodium*. The appearance of this term in one district and in one only is far from proving that there had been anything peculiar in the law of that district. It may well be a mere chance that the *liberi homines* of other counties are not called *alodiaries*. Still in Hampshire, where alodiaries abounded, it was not every free man holding land who had an *alod*. Perhaps we shall be right in thinking that the term pointed to heritability:—the free man who holds land but has no *alod* has only an estate for life. Certainly it does not mean that the tenant has no lord. The alodiary may hold his alod "of" his lord; he may owe service to his lord; he may pay a relief; he may have no power "to withdraw himself with his land" from his lord. The Norman lawyers had no speculative objection to the existence of alodiaries; it in no way contradicted such doctrine of tenure as they had formed. In 1086 there were still alodiaries in Berkshire, and in royal charters of a much later day there is talk of the alodiaries of Kent as of an existing class. It is just possible that William's commissioners saw some difference between holding *in feudo* and holding *in alodio*. If ever they contrasted the two words, they may have hinted that while the *feudum* has been given by the lord to the man, the *alodium* has been brought by the man to the lord; but we can not be very certain that they ever opposed these terms to each other. Such sparse evidence as we can obtain from Normandy strengthens our belief that the wide, the almost insuperable, gulf that modern theorists have found or have set between "alodial ownership" and "feudal tenure" was not perceptible in the eleventh century. It can be no part of our task to trace the history of these terms *alodium* and *feudum* behind the date at which they are brought into England, but hereafter we shall see that here in England a process had been at work which, had these terms been in use, would have brought the alod very near to the feud, the feud very near to the alod.

It is probable that this process had gone somewhat further in Normandy than in England. It is probable that the Normans knew that in imposing upon all English lands "the formula of dependent tenure" they were simplifying matters. They seem to think, and they may be pretty right in thinking, that every English land-holder had held his land under (*sub*) some lord; but apparently they do not think that every English land-holder had held his land of (*de*) some lord. Not unfrequently they show that this is so. Thus one Sigar holds a piece of Cambridgeshire *of* Geoffrey de Mandeville; he used to hold it *under* Aesgar the Staller. We catch a slight shade of difference between the two prepositions; *sub* lays stress on the lord's power, which may well be of a personal or justiciary, rather than of a proprietary kind, while *de* imports a theory about the origin of the tenure; it makes the tenant's rights look like derivative rights:—it is supposed that he gets his land from his lord. And at least in the eastern counties—so it may well have seemed to the Normans—matters sadly needed simplification. Even elsewhere and when a large estate is at stake they can not always get an answer to the question "Of whom was this land holden?"

III

Historical Imagination

The importance of imagination on the historian's part, if he is to make any attempt to appraise the significance of historical events, would seem to be fairly obvious. A philosopher who took a deep interest in history, the late Morris R. Cohen, *remarked that we can no more appreciate the historical significance of* Napoleon *without asking what might have happened if he had been killed in his first battle than we can appreciate the climatic significance of the inclination of the earth's axis without asking what would have happened had there been no such inclination. The kind of imagination that he had in mind is something very different from the idle and unrestrained fancy that builds castles in the air. It comes into play only in historically informed minds. The historian ought, of course, to strive to ascertain, by critical use of the authorities available to him, what actually happened. But if he is concerned with its significance, he should also ask himself what might have happened. Sometimes it is possible to find out from their recorded predictions what contemporaries thought would probably happen if some event which later occurred should not occur. But usually this is not the case, and the historian who asks himself what might have happened has to do his own conjecturing for himself. Maitland's* English Law and the Renaissance, *from which extracts are given here, illustrates a historian's exercise of the faculty of imagination. It was given as the Rede Lecture for 1901. Sir Robert Rede was an English jurist who lived in the late fifteenth and early sixteenth century; his name has been perpetuated by an annual lectureship which he endowed at Cambridge University. Maitland's opinion that the continued existence of the common law was in grave danger in the sixteenth century has not been generally accepted. Sir William Holdsworth came to the conclusion in an article published in the* Law Quarterly Review *in 1912 that while its existence was not in danger, its supremacy was in great danger.*

A few years afterwards an enlightened young humanist, of high rank and marked ability, a man who might live to be pope of Rome or might live to be king of England, was saying much evil of the sort of law that Rede had administered and taught [the English common law]; was saying that a wise prince would banish this barbaric stuff and receive in its stead the civil law of the Romans. Such, so we learn from one of his friends, was the talk of Reginald Pole, and a little knowledge of what was happening in foreign countries is enough to teach us that such talk deserves attention.

This was the time when Roman law was driving German law out of Germany or forcing it to conceal itself in humble forms and obscure corners. If this was the age of the Renaissance and the age of the Reformation, it was also the age of the "Reception." I need not say that this Reception—the reception of Roman law—plays a large part in modern versions of German history, and by no means only in such as are written by lawyers. I need not say that it has been judged from many different points of view, that it has been connected by some with political, by others with religious and by yet others with economic changes. Nor need I say that of late years few writers have had a hearty good word for the Reception. We have all of us been nationalists of late. Cosmopolitanism can afford to await its turn.

Then we observe that not long after Pole had been advocating a Reception, his cousin King Henry [VIII], whose word was law supreme in church and state, prohibited the academic study of one great and ancient body of law—the canon law—and encouraged the study of another—the civil law—by the foundation of professorships at Oxford and Cambridge. We observe also that his choice of a man to fill the chair at Cambridge fell on one who was eminently qualified to represent in his own person that triad of the three R's—Renaissance, Reformation and Reception. We know Professor Thomas Smith as a humanist, an elegant scholar with advanced opinions about the pronunciation of Greek. We know the Reverend Thomas Smith as a decided, if cautious, protestant whose doings are of some interest to those who study the changeful history of ecclesiastical affairs. Then we know Dr. Thomas Smith as a doctor in law of the university of Padua, for with praiseworthy zeal when he was appointed professor at Cambridge he journeyed to the fountain-head for his Roman law and his legal degree. Also he visited those French universities whence a new jurisprudence was beginning to spread. He returned to speak to us in two inaugural lectures of this new jurisprudence: to speak with enthusiasm of Alciatus and Zasius: to speak hopefully of the future that lay before this conquering science—the future that lay before it in an England fortunately ruled by a pious, wise, learned and munificent Prince. Then in Edward VI's day Thomas Smith as a Master of Requests was doing justice in a court whose procedure was described as being "altogether according to the process of summary causes in the civil law [i.e., Roman law]" and at that moment this Court of Requests and other courts with a like procedure seemed to have time, reason and popularity upon their side. Altogether, the Rev. Prof. Dr Sir Thomas Smith, Knt., M.P., Dean of

Carlisle, Provost of Eton, Ambassador to the Court of France and Secretary of State to Queen Elizabeth was a man of mark in an age of great events. Had some of those events been other than they were, we might now be saying of him that he played a prominent part in Renaissance, Reformation and Reception, and a part characteristic of that liberal and rational university of which he was professor, public orator and vice-chancellor.

A Reception there was not to be, nor dare I say that a Reception was what our Regius Professor or his royal patron desired. As to Smith himself, it is fairly evident that some time afterwards, when he had resigned his chair and was Elizabeth's ambassador at the French court, he was well content to contrast the public law of England with that of "France, Italy, Spain, Germany and all other countries which" to use his words "do follow the civil law of the Romans compiled by Justinian into his Pandects and Code." The little treatise on the Commonwealth of England which he wrote at Toulouse in 1565—a remarkable feat for he had no English books at hand—became a classic in the next century, and certainly did not underrate those traditional, medieval, Germanic and parliamentary elements which were still to be found in English life and law under the fifth and last of the Tudors. Nevertheless I think that a well-equipped lecturer might persuade a leisurely audience to perceive that in the second quarter of the sixteenth century the continuity of English legal history was seriously threatened.

Unquestionably our medieval law was open to humanistic attacks. It was couched partly in bad Latin, partly in worse French. For the business Latin of the middle age there is much to be said. . . . But this business Latin was a pure and elegant language when compared with what served our lawyers as French. Pole and Smith might well call it barbarous; that it was fast becoming English was its one redeeming feature.

Turning to a more serious aspect of affairs, it would not I think be difficult to show that the pathway for a Reception was prepared. Not difficult but perhaps wearisome. . . . Howbeit, we may think of the subjected church and the humbled baronage, of the parliament which exists to register the royal edicts, of the English *Lex Regia* [the name later given to an act of parliament passed under Henry VIII] which gives the force of statute to the king's proclamations, of the undeniable faults of the common law, of its dilatory methods, of bribed and perjured juries, of the new courts which grow out of the King's Council and adopt a summary procedure devised by legists and decretists. Might not the Council and the Star Chamber and the Court of Requests —courts not tied and bound by ancient formalism,— do the romanizing work that was done in Germany by the Imperial Chamber Court, the *Reichskammergericht?* This was the time when King Henry's nephew James V was establishing a new court in Scotland, a College of Justice, and Scotland was to be the scene of a Reception.

It seems fairly certain that, besides all that he effected, Henry had at times large projects in his mind: a project for a great college of law (possibly a College of Justice in the Scotch sense), a project for the reformation of the Inns of Court, which happily were not rich enough to deserve dissolution, also perhaps a project for a civil code as well as the better known project for a code ecclesiastical. In Edward VI's day our Regius and German Professor of Divinity, Dr Martin Butzer, had heard, so it seems, that such a scheme had been taken in hand, and he moved in circles that were well informed. He urged the young Josiah [Edward VI] to go forward in the good work; he denounced the barbarism of English law and (to use Bentham's word) its incognoscibility. The new ecclesiastical code, as is generally known, was never enacted; but we know equally well that the draft is in print.

And then we see that in 1535, the year in which More was done to death, the Year Books come to an end: in other words, the great stream of law reports that has been flowing for near two centuries and a half, ever since the days of Edward I, becomes discontinuous and then runs dry. The exact significance of this ominous event has never yet been duly explored; but ominous it surely is. Some words that once fell from Edmund Burke occur to us: "To put an end to reports is to put an end to the law of England." Then in 1547 just after King Henry's death a wail went up from "divers students of the common laws." The common laws, they said, were being set aside in favour of "the law civil" insomuch that the old courts had hardly any business. Ten years later, at the end of Mary's reign, we read that the judges had nothing to do but "to look about them," and that for the few practitioners in Westminster Hall there was "elbow room enough." In criminal causes that were of any political importance an examination by two or three doctors of the civil law threatened to become a normal part of our procedure. In short, I am persuaded that in the middle years of the sixteenth century and of the Tudor age the life of our ancient law was by no means lusty.

And now we may ask what opposing force, what conservative principle was there in England? National character, the genius of a people, is a wonder-working spirit which stands at the beck and call of every historian. . . . No doubt there were many differences between England and Germany, between England and France, between England and Scotland. Let us notice one difference which, if I am not mistaken, marked off England from the rest of the world. Medieval England had schools of national law.

Very rarely do we see elsewhere the academic teaching of any law that is not Roman: imperially or papally Roman. As a matter of course the universities had the two legal faculties [the Roman civil law and the ecclesiastical canon law], unless, as at Paris, the Pope excluded the legists from an ecclesiastical preserve. The voice of John Wyclif pleading that English law was the law that should be taught in English universities was a voice that for centuries cried in the wilderness. . . . But then, throughout the later middle age English law had been academically taught.

No English institutions are more distinctively English than the Inns of Court; of none is the origin more obscure. We are only now coming into possession of the documents whence their history must be gathered, and apparently we shall never know much of their first days. Unchartered, unprivileged, unendowed, without remembered founders, these groups of lawyers formed themselves and in course of time evolved a scheme of legal education: an academic scheme of the medieval sort, oral and disputatious. For good and ill that was a big achievement: a big achievement in the history of some undiscovered continents. We may well doubt whether aught else could have saved English law in the age of the Renaissance. What is distinctive of medieval England is not parliament, for we may everywhere see assemblies of Estates, nor trial by jury, for this was but slowly suppressed in France. But the Inns of Court and the Year Books that were read therein, we shall hardly find their like elsewhere. At all events let us notice that where Littleton and Fortescue lectured, there Robert Rede lectures, Thomas More lectures, Edward Coke lectures, Francis Bacon lectures, and highly technical were the lectures that Francis Bacon gave. Now it would, so I think, be difficult to conceive any scheme better suited to harden and toughen a traditional body of law than one which, while books were still uncommon, compelled every lawyer to take part in legal education and every distinguished lawyer to read public lectures. That was what I meant when I made bold to say that Robert Rede was not only an English judge but "what is more" a reader in English law.

Deus bone! exclaimed Professor Smith in his inaugural lecture, and what excited the learned doctor to this outcry was the skill in disputation shown by the students of English law in their schools at London. He was endeavouring to persuade his hearers that in many ways the study of law would improve their minds. If, he urged, these young men, cut off as they are from all the humanities, can reason thus over their "barbaric and semi-gallic laws," what might not you, you cultivated scholars do if you studied the Digest and Alciatus and Zasius? And then the professor expressed a hope that he might be able to spend his vacation in the Inns of Court. His heart was in the right place: in a school of living law. Even for the purposes of purely scientific observation the live dog may be better than the dead lion.

When the middle of the century is past the signs that English law has a new lease of life become many. The medieval books poured from the press, new books were written, the decisions of the courts were more diligently reported, the lawyers were boasting of the independence and extreme antiquity of their system. We were having a little Renaissance of our own: or a gothic revival if you please. . . . That wonderful Edward Coke was loose. The medieval tradition was more than safe in his hands. You may think it pleasant to turn from this masterful, masterless man to his great rival. It is not very safe to say what Thomas More did not know, less safe to say what was unknown to Francis Bacon, but I cannot discover that either of these scholars, these philosophers, these statesmen, these law reformers, these schemers of ideal republics, these chancellors of the realm, these law lecturers, had more than a bowing acquaintance with Roman law.

If Reginald Pole's dream had come true, if there had been a Reception—well, I have not the power to guess and you have not the time to hear what would have happened; but I think that we should have had to rewrite a great deal of history. For example, in the seventeenth century there might have been a struggle between king and parliament, but it would hardly have been that struggle for the medieval, the Lancastrian, constitution in which Coke and Selden and Prynne and other ardent searchers of mouldering records won their right to be known to school-boys. In 1610 when the conflict was growing warm a book was burnt by the common hangman: it was written by an able man in whom Cambridge should take some pride, Dr Cowell, our Regius Professor, and seemed to confirm the suspicion that Roman law and absolute monarchy went hand in hand.

The profit and loss account would be a long affair. I must make no attempt to state it. If there was the danger of barbarism and stupidity on the one side, there was the danger of pedantry on the other: the pedantry that endeavours to appropriate the law of another race and galvanizes a dead Corpus Juris into a semblance of life. . . . Let us observe, however, that much had been at stake in the little England of the sixteenth century.

IV

Textual Criticism

The extracts given below (pp. 118-125) are from Maitland's introduction to the volume he edited and published in 1884 entitled Pleas of the Crown for the County of Gloucester before the Abbot of Reading and his Fellows Justices Itinerant in the Fifth Year of the Reign of King Henry the Third and the Year of Grace 1221. *What he says about the two rolls in the Public Record Office from which he made his transcript is an illustration of textual criticism informed by historical imagination.*

The second group of extracts (pp. 125-131) are taken from Maitland's article "The 'Praerogativa Regis'," published in 1891 in the English Historical Review, VI. *Here he argues from internal evidence that a document which had been supposed to be a statute, and had been printed as a statute of Edward II, was not a statute, and that it was written during the reign of Edward I.*

There are in the Record Office two rolls containing

the Gloucestershire business of this eyre. Let them be called A and B.

The latter of these rolls is in very good condition, while in the former the lower part of almost every membrane has suffered badly. In general the damage has not gone far beyond the margin, and only some twenty or thirty cases are very seriously mutilated. Again, while B seems for the more part the work of one hand, at least some four different clerks have been employed upon A. The strips of parchment in A are in general both longer and wider than those in B, and perhaps hereafter, when a sufficient number of rolls have been examined, this fact may prove to be of some significance.

The relation between these two rolls is intricate and curious. The parts of them which contain pleas of the crown have been carefully compared. In general they agree word for word, and that too both in what seem to be blunders and in some very strange phrases, literal translations of English colloquialisms, and the like. Again, in both there are what shall be called *postscripts,* that is to say, the clerk, having carried his report of a case to a certain point, has passed on to another case, and afterwards he, or some other clerk, has gone back to the former case and added some new facts, the verdict of a jury or the like. In many instances the fact that a passage is postscript is very obvious, for the scribe had not left enough room for the additional materials and was put to shifts for space. What is clearly postscript in one of the rolls is generally postscript also in the other. Further, when a phrase has been introduced into one by interlineation, a similar interlineation is often found in the other; when a word has been struck out in one it has often been struck out in the other also; when the erasing knife has been used on the one it has sometimes been used on the other also.

But while the agreement about words is generally perfect, in spelling there is great divergence. This may be noticed even in common words; but as to names of places in no way famous the two rolls as often as not disagree about the spelling of them, and sometimes the variance is very marked indeed. Apparently the scribe of each roll was in this matter quite dependent on his ear.

Again, the verbal agreement is not perfect. Generally it is quite perfect in the report of any story, whether told by jurors or litigants, and for some most curious turns of phrase we have the authority of both rolls. On the other hand, in the common forms of judgment and the like there is habitual but immaterial divergence; thus one clerk will, for a while, steadily write *judicium murdrum,* the other, *et ideo murdrum;* one, *exigatur et utlagetur,* the other, *interrogetur et utlagetur;* in A the phrase *de nocte* is very common, in B it is almost always represented by *noctu.*

But from time to time the divergence between the two goes beyond these small matters. One roll will supply some fact or some bit of reasoning not to be found in the other, and though in general it is A that gives the fuller report, still this is not always the case, and B occasionally supplies what is lacking in A.

Lastly, there are some instances in which the order of the entries in A differs from that in B. Among the pleas of the crown this is mostly found in connection with a statement that the jurors are in mercy for concealing pleas (*pro concelamento loquelarum*), and it looks as if each clerk had introduced the belated presentments where he could best find room. In the parts of the rolls which contain civil pleas there seems to be still greater disagreement as to the order in which the cases shall be introduced, and it is not improbable that the introductory matter of the cases which were going to be heard was sometimes written down before the proceedings in court took place; thus the clerk had mapped out his roll by writing e.g. "the assize comes to testify whether William disseised Roger; the jurors say," before the jurors had said anything, and then, as the jurors brought in their testimonies, the gaps which had been left were filled up.

The most plausible theory therefore as to the relation between these two rolls is, that neither was copied from the other, but that the two were kept by clerks sitting side by side, whose duty it was to produce records perfectly harmonious about all matters of importance. The spelling of a local name was of no importance; whether one should write *exigatur* or *interrogetur* was of no importance: but it was of great importance that the rolls should agree about the very words of witnesses, parties, jurors.

With regard to the postscripts it should be observed that, with one exception (an account of duels at Hereford and Worcester, found in B but not in A), nothing has been written on the roll of crown pleas that may not have been written in Gloucestershire. Among the civil pleas there are a few cases of later postscripts from Hereford, Worcester, and even from Westminster. As a rule, however, there seems to have been no attempt to "make up a record," i.e. to present continuously the successive stages of each case. Only what happens in Gloucestershire is put on this roll, though it may be no more than that the parties are adjourned to Hereford or to Westminster.

There is therefore little to choose between these two rolls. But on the whole A, though mutilated, seems rather the more worthy to be the subject of a transcript. In the first place it gives us, and B does not, the list of amercements, which is of great value, if we are to have a complete picture of the eyre; and in the second place the main part of this roll has apparently been used in the drawing up of this list of amercements. In A there are not a few cases in which the text states that so and so is *in misericordia*, and the abbreviation $\overline{mia}$ is duly entered in the margin; but afterwards a pen has been drawn through this symbol, and occasionally a reason is given why there is to be no amercement: the person is dead (*obiit*), or is poor (*pauper*), or is pardoned (*perdonatur*), or, for some reason or another, is not to be fined (*nichil*). These marks and notes are much more frequent in A than in B and suggest that, when the time for assessing the amercements came, the former roll was used as the basis of the work and the body of that roll was brought into harmony with the list of amercements by a process of correction. So again postscripts are more common in A than in B; for instance, when both rolls have told us that John is to be kept in custody (*custodiatur*), A will add that afterwards he made fine (*finem fecit*); apparently therefore A has been posted up to the end of the Gloucestershire session, and we have in it the very latest intelligence. Lastly, it may be noticed that amongst the civil pleas A has several enrolled instruments, deeds of grant and the like, which B has not. Again, it records the election of the coroners, which B does not. It looks therefore as if A was the roll which was to be kept in the treasury; the roll which would check the sheriff's accounts; the roll to which a litigant might hereafter appeal as establishing some matter of record. On the other hand, B may be a roll belonging to the judges in general, or to some judge in particular.

And now the transcriber must give an account of

his doings. I have copied from A when A was legible, and when the margin of A was damaged so that an entry on that roll wanted but a few words to make it perfect, the corresponding words have been supplied from B. I wish now that I had more carefully noted the exact amount of help derived in this way from B, but it has been small. Whenever the entry in A was at all seriously mutilated, the corresponding entry has been copied from B, and the entries thus taken from B may be known by the [B] placed before them in the text.

In the foot-notes attention is drawn to the material differences between A and B, material, that is, in a lawyer's view; but of merely verbal or literal differences I have in general made no note. This transcript does not profess to be worthy of any philologist's or grammarian's attention. If these rolls are worth editing as specimens of medieval Latin (their value as such must, I should imagine, be very small), they must be edited by some one much more learned than I am.

It is a difficult question how such a document as this is best transcribed and printed. On the one hand, absolute fidelity seems to require the use of type which shall, as far as possible, reproduce the marks of abbreviation which are very freely used in the original. But such type is repulsive to modern eyes, the use of it is expensive, and, after all, though it may confine the transcriber's chances of blundering within somewhat narrower limits, it still leaves a large room wherein his ignorance and carelessness may display themselves. In this case again the document itself is in the safest custody and is easily accessible to most of those who would really care to read a facsimile of it. Therefore the most opposite course has been taken, and I have endeavoured to write out in full every abbreviated word. This certainly has given me abundant opportunities for making mistakes of many kinds. The abbreviated words are very numerous, and the clerks in their haste have made great use not only of the regular stenographic signs, each of which has a specific meaning, but also of the indiscriminating dash, which, when drawn over the end of a word, may stand for almost any termination. It is not improbable that in many cases these have been misinterpreted, especially when the abbreviated word is the name of a place. To make a first-rate copy of such a role as this would require knowledge of many kinds, grammatical, etymological, historical, geographical, antiquarian, to which I can make no claim (*et ideo in misericordia*); it must be enough if I have not misrepresented matters of law.

Dr. E. F. Henderson has raised an interesting question, and one which, if I am not mistaken, has never received that full discussion which it deserves. What is the date and what is the nature of the document which passes under the title "Praerogativa Regis"? It used to be printed as a statute of the seventeenth year of Edward II. This, as I believe, was due to a mere accident. The lawyers of the later middle ages in their manuscripts drew a line between the "Statuta Vetera," which ended with the end of Edward II's reign, and the "Statuta Nova," which began with the beginning of Edward III's reign. Between the two, like an apocrypha between the two testaments, they inserted a group of documents about the date and the character of which they were uncertain, and among these documents the "Praerogativa Regis." Then, when the time for printing had come, the position in which these documents were found gave rise to the inference that they were statutes of some year late in the reign of Edward II. Now to this inference there is an objection which seems insuperable. A statute of Edward II's reign—an important statute, if statute it were—would be upon the statute roll; but the "Praerogativa Regis" is not upon the statute roll, but has to be discovered in mere private manuscripts. Therefore I can agree with Dr. Henderson when he rejects this date, but when he would make the document in question a statute of Henry III's reign then I most respectfully differ from him. It seems to me no statute, but a tract written by some lawyer in the early years of Edward I. May I be allowed to say a few words in defence of this opinion?

In the first place, throughout the whole document there is no word of command, nothing about "ordaining" or "establishing," nothing about "I" or "we," no reference to the quarter from which it proceeds. It is just an objective statement of the king's rights; the king shall have this, the king shall have that. Was ever any other English statute couched in such a form? I think not. Another question: Does any other statute condescend to tell stories? Here we have a story about the heirs of John of Monmouth (c. 14), and another story about the widow of Anselm Marshall (c. 15). But let us look at the matter more closely, taking as our guides Bracton, who wrote somewhere about 1255, Britton and Fleta, who wrote somewhere about 1290.

The first seven chapters afford me no matter for remark, save that in the fourth there is mention of "King Henry, father of King Edward." How Dr. Henderson would deal with this passage I cannot guess; perhaps he regards it as an interpolation, for he can hardly endow Henry III with a spirit of prophecy. To my mind this passage tells us plainly that the document was written after Henry's death, and also, though less plainly, that it was written during the life of his son.

The eighth and ninth chapters deal with alienations made by the king's tenants in chief and state a doctrine intermediate between that of Bracton on the one hand and that of Britton and Fleta on the other. It would be long to discuss this matter minutely, but the subjoined references[1] will show that while in Bracton the king's claim to check the alienations made by his tenants in chief goes hardly beyond the well-known provision of the charter of 1217, Britton has nearly and Fleta has quite arrived at the broad principle of later law—namely, that no tenant in chief of the crown can alienate the whole or any part of his tenement without the king's consent. Now in this respect our "Praerogativa" stands nearer to Bracton than to Fleta. No one who holds of the king in chief *by military service* may alienate *the greater part* of his land without royal license; "but this is not wont to be understood" concerning "members and parcels of the same lands." Raising by the way the question whether statutes often tell us what "is wont to be understood," I here find a reason for saying that this document lies between Bracton and Fleta.

The eleventh chapter introduces a very curious topic, the king's rights in the lands of "natural fools." I believe that of these very valuable rights there is no trace in Bracton; on the other hand Britton and Fleta know them well, and so far as my knowledge goes they begin to appear in the reign of Edward I.

In its fourteenth chapter we have a story from Henry III's reign. John of Monmouth died; his heir was an alien, a Breton, and King Henry took his land. In the fifteenth we have another story from

[1] Bracton, f. 169*b*, 395; Britton, i. 222; Fleta, p. 178.

the same reign. On the death of William, Earl Marshall, his brother and heir, Anselm, entered on the lands that had descended to him without first doing homage to the king; he then died, and it was adjudged that his widow, Maud, daughter of the earl of Hereford, should have no dower, for her husband had entered as an intruder on the king. John of Monmouth I take to be the bearer of that name who died in or shortly before 1257; he seems to have left as heiresses two aunts, who were of the family of Waleran. The tale about the Marshalls is not quite correctly told by this so-called statute. The inheritance did not pass immediately from William to Anselm; as is well known it came to five brothers in succession, of whom William was the eldest and Anselm the youngest; Anselm died in 1245, and his widow, Maud, died in or shortly before 1252. These stories about what happened in the middle of the thirteenth century would hardly have been very interesting to lawyers in the fourteenth, when they would have been regarded as antiquated illustrations of well-established legal rules. That Edward II's parliament was at pains to tell them I should not easily believe.

We come to the chapter on which Dr. Henderson relies. The king is to have year, day, and waste of the felon's land; the tenement is to be actually wasted. Britton mentions the wasting as a thing of the past; upon this Dr. Henderson founds an argument that the "Praerogativa" comes from Henry III's day. But why, I must ask, may it not come from the early years of Edward I? Britton did not write until 1290 or thereabouts; at least his book as we have it was not written until then. This leaves some seventeen years during which the change in the law, if change there was, may have taken place, without our being driven to suppose that a document which mentions King Edward was written before his accession.

In Edward III's reign those who held that the "Praerogativa" was a statute believed it to be a statute of Edward I; but there were others who said that it was no statute at all, but a mere "rehearsal" of the common law. Throughout the middle ages it never obtained an unconditional acceptance as part of the written law of England. In 1475 all the great lawyers seem agreed that it is no statute. Littleton in particular is clear and emphatic. It is an "affirmance of the common law, for every statute mentions the date at which it was made, but this document is dateless; it is not a statute. . . . Then Littleton tells how "my lord Markham" had disregarded the words of the "Praerogativa," and so, he repeats once more, "it cannot be called a statute." What exactly these judges meant when they said that the document was a "rehearsal" or an "affirmance" of the common law is not in all cases very plain. . . . Littleton very probably thought that great respect was due to the "Praerogativa"; it was a venerable statement of common law, and perhaps he believed that it had been issued by some person or body of persons having power to make statements of law which should command the respect of the justices; but certainly he did not think that its very words were law as the very words of a statute would be law. Markham had disregarded them, and Littleton was ready to do the like.

Whether it be purely private work or no I will not take on me to decide; it may have been a document issued by the king to his serjeants, possibly to his judges, instructing them as to the king's views of his own rights (at every doubtful point it leans towards royal claims); but at least I think that we ought to agree with Littleton, *ceo ne poet estre dit come un statute.*

V

Why the History of English Law Was Not Written

In Maitland's inaugural lecture in 1888 as Downing Professor of the Laws of England at Cambridge, which is here reprinted in part, he gave the reasons that explained to his mind why no adequate history of English law had been written. The only book then in existence which dealt with the subject as a whole was the work of John Reeves, the successive volumes of which (five in all) were published in the late eighteenth and the early nineteenth century, and it did not come this side of the Tudor period. Maitland elsewhere paid his respects to Reeves for his patience and industry, as later historians of English law have done, but Reeves's book, as one of them has said, is "incredibly dull," and the early history of the common law remained, in the words of Sir Frederick Pollock, "obscure, insulated, a seeming chaos of technical antiquities." Maitland was evidently in despondent mood about the future of English legal history as a field of study when he delivered this "dismal discourse," as he called it. (This lecture was first published in 1911 and appears in his Collected Papers *edited by H. A. L. Fisher.)*

And now why is our history unwritten? In the first place, I think we may say, because of the traditional isolation of the study of English law from every other study, an isolation which is illustrated by the fact that it is only of late years, late years to us who have been dealing in centuries, that English law has had a home in the Universities. In 1850 when my predecessor Professor Amos came to the chair, the class of English law in this University consisted of one M.A., one B.A. and two undergraduates. At another time it may be interesting to account for this, to observe the formation of law schools in London while the Universities are teaching to ever fewer students a kind of law, Roman and Canon Law, which is not the law of the King's Courts, and becomes of ever less and less importance to the bulk of Englishmen. This process had momentous results and, all things considered, we cannot regret them. If the Universities had taught English law, English law would sooner or later have ceased to be English. But as it was, the education of the English lawyer—I speak of the later middle ages and of the Tudor time—was not academic; it was scholastic. It would be a great mistake to suppose that the lawyers of that age got their law in the haphazard hand-to-mouth fashion that is familiar to us under the name of "reading in chambers." They went through an elaborate scholastic course which if not severe was at least prolonged—ten or twelve years of "readings," "mootings" and "boltings," of hearing and giving lectures, and the path of scholastic success was the path to profit and to place. The law which this school evolved stood us in good stead: it was the bridge which carried us safely from medieval to modern times and we will speak well of it. But one thing it could not do, it could not possibly produce its own historian. History involves comparison and the English lawyer who knew nothing and cared nothing for any system but his own hardly came in sight of the idea of legal history. And when the old scholastic plan of education broke down no other plan took its place. It is hardly too much to say that nobody taught law or attempted to teach it, and that no one studied law save with the most purely practical intentions. Whatever may be the advantages of such a mode of study it will never issue in a written history of English law.

The one great law book of the last century may serve to illustrate two points, though I have some hesitation about mentioning the first of them. Blackstone's work was the firstfruits of a professorship of law; in the presence of that book every professor of law will always feel very small, but there it stands the imperishable monument of what may be done by obliging a lawyer to teach law. But in the second place let us take one of Blackstone's greatest exploits, his statement of our land-law and of its history. Every one now-a-days can pick holes in "the feudal system" and some great writers can hardly mention it without loss of temper. But the theory of a feudal system it was that enabled Blackstone to paint his great picture, a picture incomplete and with many faults in it, but the first picture ever painted. Whence did he get the theory which made this possible? From Coke? Coke had no such theory and because he had none was utterly unable to give any connected account of the law that he knew so well. No, the feudal system was a very early essay in comparative jurisprudence, and the man who had the chief part in introducing the feudal system into England was Henry Spelman. It was the idea of a law common to all the countries of Western Europe that enabled Blackstone to achieve the task of stating English law in a rational fashion. And so it will be found during the length of our national life; an isolated system cannot explain itself, still less explain its history. When great work has been done some fertilizing germ has been wafted from abroad; now it may be the influence of Azo and now of the Lombard feudists, now of Savigny and now of Brunner. Let me not be misunderstood:—there is not much "comparative jurisprudence" for those who do not know thoroughly well the things to be compared, not much "comparative jurisprudence" for Englishmen who will not slave at their law reports; but still there is nothing that sets a man thinking and writing to such good effect about a system of law and its history as an acquaintance however slight with other systems and their history. One of the causes why so little has been done for our medieval law is I feel sure our very complete and traditionally consecrated ignorance of French and German law. English lawyers have for the last six centuries exaggerated the uniqueness of our legal history by overrating and antedating the triumphs of Roman law upon the continent. I know just enough to say this with confidence, that there are great masses of medieval law very comparable with our own; a little knowledge of them would send us to our Year Books with new vigour and new intelligence.

In the second place it may seem a paradox, but I think it true, that the earlier ages of English law are so little studied because all English lawyers are expected to know something about them. In his first text-book the student is solemnly warned that he must know the law as it stood in Edward I's day, and unfortunately it is quite impossible to write the simplest book about our land-law without speaking of the *De Donis* and the *Quia Emptores.* Well, a stranger might exclaim, what a race of medievalists you English lawyers ought to be! But on enquiry we shall find that the practical necessity for a little knowledge is a positive obstacle to the attainment of more knowledge and also that what is really required of the practising lawyer is not, save in the rarest cases, a knowledge of medieval law as it was in the middle ages, but rather a knowledge of medieval law as interpreted by modern courts to suit modern facts. A lawyer finds on his table a case about rights of common which sends him to the Statute of Merton. But is it really the law of 1236 that he wants to know? No, it is the ultimate result of the interpretations set on the statute by the judges of twenty generations. The more modern the decision the more valuable for his purpose. That process by which old principles and old phrases are charged with a new content, is from the lawyer's point of view an evolution of the true intent and meaning of the old law; from the historian's point of view it is almost of necessity a process of perversion and misunderstanding. Thus we are tempted to mix up two different logics, the logic of authority, and the logic of evidence. What the lawyer wants is authority and the newer the better; what the historian wants is evidence and the older the better. This when stated is obvious; but often we conceal it from ourselves under some phrase about "the common law." It is possible to find in modern books comparisons between what Bracton says and what Coke says about the law as it stood before the statutes of Edward I, and the writer of course tells us that Coke's is "the better opinion." Now if we want to know the common law of our own day Coke's authority is higher than Bracton's and Coke's own doctrines yield easily to modern decisions. But if we are really looking for the law of Henry III's reign, Bracton's lightest word is infinitely more valuable than all the tomes of Coke. A mixture of legal dogma and legal history is in general an unsatisfactory compound. I do not say that there are not judgments and text-books which have achieved the difficult task of combining the results of deep historical research with luminous and accurate exposition of existing law—neither confounding the dogma nor perverting the history; but the task is difficult. The lawyer must be orthodox otherwise he is no lawyer; an orthodox history seems to me a contradiction in terms. If this truth is hidden from us by current phrases about "historical methods of legal study," that is another reason why the history of our law is unwritten. If we try to make history the handmaid of dogma she will soon cease to be history.

Macaulay in an amusing passage, amusing because it comes from him, has told us how "the historical literature of England has suffered grievously from a circumstance which has not a little contributed to her prosperity. . . . A Frenchman," he says, "is not now compelled by any strong interest either to exaggerate or to underrate the power of the kings of the house of Valois. . . . The gulph of a great revolution completely separates the new from the old system. No such chasm divides the existence of the English nation into two distinct parts. . . . With us the precedents of the middle ages are still valid precedents and are still cited on the gravest occasions by the most eminent statesmen. . . . In our country the dearest interests of parties have frequently been staked on the researches of antiquaries. The inevitable consequence was that our antiquaries conducted their researches in the spirit of partisans." Well, that reproach has passed away; but the manipulation which was required to make the political precedents of the middle ages serve the turn of Whig or Tory was a coarse and obvious distortion when compared with the subtle process against which the historian of our law will have to be on his guard, the subtle process whereby our common law has gradually accommodated itself to changed circumstances. I make no doubt that it is easier for a Frenchman or a German to study medieval law than it is for an Englishman; he has not before his mind the fear that he is saying what is not "practically sound," that he may seem to be unsettling the law or usurping the functions of a judge. There are many good reasons for wishing that some parts of our law, notably our land-law, were thoroughly purged of their archaisms; of these reasons it is needless to say anything; but I am sure that the study of legal history would not suffer thereby. I do not ask for "the gulph of a great revolution"; but it is to the interest of the middle ages themselves that they be not brought into court any more.

Are we to say then that the study of modern law and the study of legal history have nothing to do with each other? That would be an exaggeration; but it is true and happily true that a man may be an excellent lawyer and know little of the remoter parts of history. We can not even say that every sound lawyer will find an interest in them; many will; some will not. But we can say this, that a thorough training in modern law is almost indispensable for any one who wishes to do good work on legal history. In whatever form the historian of law may give his results to the world—and the prejudice against beginning at the end is strong if unreasonable—he will often have to work from the modern to the ancient, from the clear to the vague, from the known to the unknown. Of course he must work forwards as well as backwards; the stream must be traced downwards as well as upwards; but the lower reaches are already mapped and by studying the best maps of them he will learn where to look for the sources. Again I do not think that an Englishman will often have the patience to study medieval procedure and conveyancing unless he has had to study modern procedure and modern conveyancing and to study them professionally.

This brings us to the heart of the matter. The only persons in this country who possess very fully one of the great requisites for the work are as a rule very unlikely to attempt it. They are lawyers with abundant practice or hopes of abundant practice; if they have the taste they have not the time, the ample leisure, that is necessary for historical research.

What then can the Universities do? Pardon me if I say that I do not answer this question very cheerfully. In the first place, the object of a law school must be to teach law, and this is not quite the same thing as teaching the history of law. We should not wish to see a professor of law breaking and entering the close of the professor of history, though the result of our scheme of Triposes may be that legal history falls to the ground between two schools. Secondly, I believe that any one who aspires to study legal history should begin by studying modern law. Could we dispose of the time and energies of the young man who is destined—surely he is born by this time—to tell the story of English law, we should advise him to pursue some such course of reading as that prescribed for our Tripos, to go into chambers and into court, even to do what in him lies to acquire some small practice; many other things he should do, but these should not be left undone. Thirdly, the time that we have at our command is exceedingly short. We can not reckon that an undergraduate will give so much as two years to English law, and what he can learn in two years is not very much, regard being had to the enormous scope of our modern law. Fourthly, our students are many and teachers are few. Thus I have come to the conclusion, reluctantly for I have had my dreams, that in the ordinary teaching of our law school there is very little room for history, hardly any for remote history. At the same time every effort should be made which can possibly have the result of inducing a few students, those who will have taste and leisure for the work, to turn their thoughts towards the great neglected subject. They might at least learn to know where the evidence lies. May I mention my own case? I had not the advantage of studying law at Cambridge, otherwise perhaps I should not have been a barrister of seven years' standing before I had any idea of the whereabouts of the first-hand evidence for the law of the middle ages. It were to be wished that we had more prizes like the Yorke prize; already it has done more for the cause than any Tripos could do. It were to be wished that our doctor's degree had all along been reserved for those who had done some considerable thing for law or legal history:—but then what could we have done for potentates and politicians and such? Impossible to convict them of divinity or medicine, it was convenient to fall back on the legal principle that every one must be taken to know the law sufficiently well to be a doctor thereof.

Where then lies our trust? Perhaps in failure. Failure is not a pleasant word to use in the presence of youth and hope; it would be pleasanter to wish all our law students success in their chosen profession. But let us look facts in the face. Only a few of the men who choose that profession succeed in it: the qualities which make a man a great lawyer are rare and the space on the wool-sack is strictly limited. The Cambridge law student should be prepared for either fortune. The day may come when in the bitterness of his soul he will confess that he is not going to succeed, when he is weary of waiting for that solicitor who never comes, when the prolonged and costly education seems thrown away. That is the hopeful moment; that is the moment when something that has been said here may bear its fruit. Far be it from us to suggest that there is but one outgo from the dismal situation; there are many things that a man can do the better because he knows some law. But in that day of tribulation may it be remembered that the history of English law has not been written. Perhaps our imaginary student is not he that should come, not the great man for the great book. To be frank with him, this is probable; great historians are at least as rare as great lawyers. But short of the very greatest work, there is good work to be done of many sorts and kinds, large provinces to be reclaimed from the waste, to be settled and cultivated for the use of man. Let him at least know that within a quarter of a mile of the chambers in which he sits lies the most glorious store of material for legal history that has ever been collected in one place, and it is free to all like the air and the sunlight. At least he can copy, at least he can arrange, digest, make serviceable. Not a very splendid occupation and we can not promise him much money or much fame—though let it be confessed that such humble work has before now been extravagantly rewarded. He may find his reward in the work itself: —one can not promise him even that; but the work ought to be done and the great man when he comes may fling a foot-note of gratitude to those who have smoothed his way, who have saved his eyes and his time.

At the end of this long and dismal discourse let me tell a story. It is said that long ago a certain professor of English law was also the chief justice of an ancient episcopal franchise. It is said that one of his rulings was cited in the court presided over by a chief justice of a more august kind, the Lord Chief Justice of England. "Did he rule that?" said my lord, "why he is only fit to rule a copy-book." Well, I will not say that this pedagogic function is all that should be expected of a professor of law; but still copy-books there ought to be and I would gladly spend much time in ruling them, if I thought that they were to be filled to the greater glory of the history of English law.

VI

Interpretation of Anglo-Saxon Land Books and Charters

Although published more than sixty years ago, Domesday Book and Beyond, *from which the following selections have been taken, has continued to be of inspirational value to more recent scholarship in Anglo-Saxon economic, social, and legal history. Maitland's ideas about the early Anglo-Saxon land books attracted wide attention.*

No one can spend patient hours in examining the complex web disclosed by Domesday Book without making some theories, at least some guesses, about the political, social and economic threads of which that web has been woven But if we here venture to fashion and state a few such theories or such guesses, it is with no hope that they will be a complete explanation of old English history. For, in the first place, we are to speak mainly of the things of the law, of legal ideas and legal forms, and once for all we may protest that we have no wish to overestimate their importance. The elaborate and long continued development to which we point when we speak of "feudalism," can not be fully explained by any discussion of legal ideas and legal forms. On the other hand, it can not be fully explained without such discussion, for almost all that we can know about it is to be found in legal documents. In the second place, we are to make a selection. Certain phases of our oldest legal history, notably those which are called "constitutional," have been so fully treated by classical books, that at the present moment there is no good reason why we should traverse the ground that has been covered. Therefore if, for example, we say little or nothing of the ancient Germanic *comitatus* or of the relationship between lord and man in so far as it is a merely personal relationship, this will not be because we have overlooked these matters; it will be because there is nothing to be gained by our repeating what has been well and sufficiently said by Dr Konrad Maurer, Dr Reinhold Schmid, Dr Stubbs and others. And if, again, we lay great stress on what may be called the ecclesiastical phase of the feudalizing process, this will not be because we think it the only phase, it will be because we think that too little attention has been paid by English writers to the influence which the churches exercised upon temporal affairs by means of their endowments. The day for an artistically proportioned picture of the growth of feudalism has not yet come; the day for a quantitave analysis of the elements of feudalism may never come; for the present we must be content if we can bring out a few new truths or set a few old truths in a new light. The vast and intricate subject may be approached from many different quarters. If we can make some little progress along our chosen path, we shall be all the more willing to admit that progress along other paths is possible.

It can not but be, however, that this part of our work should be controversial, though it need not be polemical. We are told that "in spite of all the labour that has been spent on the early history of England, scholars are still at variance upon the most fundamental of questions: the question whether that history began with a population of independent freemen or with a population of dependent serfs." Some exception may be taken to this statement. No one denies that for the purposes of English history slavery is a primitive institution, nor that in the seventh and eighth centuries there were many slaves in England. On the other hand, no one will assert that we can ascertain, even approximately, the ratio that the number of slaves bore to the number of free men. Moreover such terms as "dependent" and "independent" are not words that we can profitably quarrel over, since they are inexact and ambiguous. For all this, however, it may well be said that there are two main theories before the world. The one would trace the English manor back to the Roman villa, would think of the soil of England as being tilled from the first mainly by men who, when they were not mere slaves, were *coloni* ascript to the land. The other would postulate the existence of a large number of free men who with their own labour tilled their own soil, of men who might fairly be called free "peasant proprietors" since they were far from rich and had few slaves or servants, and yet who were no mere peasants since they habitually bore arms in the national host. What may be considered for the moment as a variant on this latter doctrine would place the ownership of the soil, or of large tracts of the soil, not in these free peasants taken as individuals, but in free village communities.

Now we will say at once that the first of these theories we can not accept if it be put forward in a general form, if it be applied to the whole or anything like the whole of England. Certainly we are not in a position to deny that in some cases, a Roman villa having come into the hands of a Saxon chieftain, he treated the slaves and *coloni* that he found upon it in much the same way as that in which they had been theretofore treated, though even in such a case the change was in all probability momentous, since large commerce and all that large commerce implies had perished. But against the hypothesis that this was the general case the English language and the names of our English villages are the unanswered protest. It seems incredible that the bulk of the population should have been of Celtic blood and yet that the Celtic language should not merely have disappeared, but have stamped few traces of itself upon the speech of the conquerors. This we regard as an objection which goes to the root of the whole matter and which throws upon those who would make the English nation in the main a nation of Celtic bondmen, the burden of strictly proving their thesis. The German invaders must have been numerous. The Britons were no cowards. They contested the soil inch by inch. The struggle was long and arduous. What then, we must ask, became of the mass of the victors? Surely it is impossible that they at once settled down as the "dependent serfs" of their chieftains. Again, though it is very likely that where we find a land of scattered steads and of isolated hamlets, there the Germanic conquerors have spared or have been unable to subdue the Britons or have adapted their own arrangements to the exterior framework that was provided by Celtic or Roman agriculture, still . . . we are compelled to say that our true villages, the nucleated villages with large "open fields," are not Celtic, are not Roman, but are very purely and typically German. But this is not all. Hereafter we shall urge some other objections. The doctrine in question will give no rational explanation of the state of things that is revealed to us by the Domesday Survey of the northern and eastern counties and it will give no rational explanation of seignorial justice. This being so, we seem bound to suppose that at one time there was a large class of peasant proprietors, that is, of free men who tilled the soil that they owned, and to discuss the process which substitutes for peasant proprietorship the manorial organization.

Though we can not deal at any length with a matter which lies outside the realm of legal history, we ought at once to explain that we need not regard this change as a retrogression. There are indeed historians who have not yet abandoned the habit of speaking of feudalism as though it were a disease of the body politic. Now the word "feudalism" is and always will be an inexact term, and, no doubt, at various times and places there emerge phenomena which may with great propriety be called feudal and which come of evil and make for evil. But if we use the term, and often we do, in a very wide sense, if we describe several centuries as feudal, then feudalism will appear to us as a natural and even a necessary stage in our history: that is to say, if we would have the England of the sixteenth century arise out of the England of the eighth without passing through a period of feudalism, we must suppose many immense and fundamental changes in the nature of man and his surroundings. If we use the term in this wide sense, then (the barbarian conquests being given us as an unalterable fact) feudalism means civilization, the separation of employments, the division of labour, the possibility of national defence, the possibility of art, science, literature and learned leisure; the cathedral, the scriptorium, the library, are as truly the work of feudalism as is the baronial castle. When therefore we speak, as we shall have to speak, of forces which make for the subjection of the peasantry to seignorial justice and which substitute the manor with its villeins for the free village, we shall—so at least it seems to us—be speaking not of abnormal forces, not of retrogression, not of disease, but in the main of normal and healthy growth. Far from us indeed is the cheerful optimism which refuses to see that the process of civilization is often a cruel process; but the England of the eleventh century is nearer to the England of the nineteenth than is the England of the seventh—nearer by just four hundred years.

This leads to a remark which concerns us more deeply. As regards the legal ideas in which feudalism is expressed a general question may be raised. If we approach them from the standpoint of modern law, if we approach them from the standpoint of the classical Roman law, they are confused ideas. In particular no clear line is drawn between public and private law. Ownership is *dominium;* but governmental power, jurisdictional power, these also are *dominium.* Office is property; taxes are rents; governmental relationships arise *ex contractu.* Then within the province of private law the ideas are few; these few have hard work to do; their outlines are blurred. One *dominium* rises above another *dominium,* one seisin over another seisin. Efforts after precision made in comparatively recent times by romanizing lawyers serve only to show how vague was the subject-matter with which they had to deal. They would give the lord a *dominium directum*, the vassal a *dominium utile;* but then, when there has been further subinfeudation, this vassal will have a *dominium utlie* as regards the lord paramount, but a *dominium directum* as regards the sub-vassal. So again, as we shall see hereafter, the gift of land shades off into the "loan" of land, the "loan" into the gift. The question then occurs whether we are right in applying to this state of things such a word as "confusion," a word which implies that things that once were distinct have wrongfully or unfortunately been mixed up with each other, a word which implies error or retrogression.

Now, no doubt, from one point of view, namely that of universal history, we do see confusion and retrogression. Ideal possessions which have been won for mankind by the thought of Roman lawyers are lost for a long while and must be recovered painfully. Lines that have been traced with precision are smudged out, and then they must be traced once more. If we regard western Europe as a whole, this retrogression appears as a slow change. How slow—that is a much controverted question. There are, for example, historians who would have us think of the Gaul of Merovingian times as being in the main governed by Roman ideas and institutions, which have indeed been sadly debased, but still are the old ideas and institutions. There are other historians who can discover in this same Gaul little that is not genuinely German and barbarous. But at any rate, it must be admitted that somehow or another a retrogression takes place, that the best legal ideas of the ninth and tenth centuries are not so good, so modern, as those of the third and fourth. If, however, we take a narrower view and fix our eyes upon the barbarian hordes which invade a Roman province, shall we say that their legal thought gradually goes to the bad, and loses distinctions which it has once apprehended? To turn to our own case—Shall we say that Englishmen of the eighth century mark the line that divides public from private law, while Englishmen of the eleventh century can not perceive it?

No one perhaps to such a question would boldly say: Yes. And yet, when it comes to a treatment of particulars, an affirmative answer seems to be implied in much that has been written even by modern historians. They begin at the beginning and attribute precise ideas and well-defined law to the German conquerors of Britain. If they began with the eleventh century and thence turned to the earlier time, they might come to another opinion, to the opinion that in the beginning all was very vague, and that such clearness and precision as legal thought has attained in the days of the Norman Conquest has been very gradually attained and is chiefly due to the influence which the old heathen world working through the Roman church has exercised upon the new. The process that is started when barbarism is brought into contact with civilization is not simple. The hitherto naked savage may at once assume some part of the raiment, perhaps the hat, of the white man. When after a while he puts these things aside and learns to make for himself clothes suitable to the climate in which he lives and the pursuits in which he is engaged, we see in this an advance, not a relapse; and yet he has abandoned some things that belong to the white man. Even so when our kings of the eighth century set their hands to documents written in Latin and bristling with the technical terms of Roman law, to documents which at first sight seem to express clear enough ideas of ownership and alienation, we must not at once assume that they have grasped these ideas. In course of time men will evolve formulas which will aptly fit their thought, for example, the "feudal" charter of feoffment with its *tenendum de me* and its *reddendo mihi*. Externally it will not be so Roman or (we may say it) so modern a document as was the land-book of the eighth century, and yet in truth there has been progress not retrogress. Words that Roman lawyers would have understood give way before words which would have been nonsense to them, *feoffamentum, liberatio seisinae* and the like. This is as it should be. Men are learning to say what they really mean.

And now let us remember that our materials for the legal history of the long age which lies behind Domesday Book are scanty. A long age it is, even if we measure it only from the date of Augustin's mission. The Conqueror stands midway between Aethelbert and Elizabeth. To illustrate five hundred years of legal history we have only the dooms and the land-books. The dooms are so much taken up with the work of keeping the peace and punishing theft that they tell us little of the structure of society or of the feudalizing process, while as to what they imply it is but too easy for different men to form different opinions. Some twelve hundred land-books or charters, genuine and spurious, are our best, almost our only, evidence, and it must needs be that they will give us but a partial and one-sided view of intricate and many-sided facts.

Book-land and the Land-book

Now these charters or land-books are, with hardly any exceptions, ecclesiastical title-deeds. Most of them are deeds whereby lands were conveyed to the churches; some are deeds whereby lands were conveyed to men who conveyed them to the churches. Partial, one-sided and in details untrustworthy though the testimony that they bear may be, there is still one general question that they ought to answer and we ought to ask. Domesday Book shows us many of the churches as the lords of wide and continuous tracts of land. Now about this important element in the feudal structure the land-books ought to tell us something. They ought to tell us how the churches acquired their territories; they ought to tell us what class of men made gifts of land to the churches; they ought to tell us whether those gifts were of big tracts or of small pieces. For example, let us remember how Domesday Book shows us that four minsters, Worcester, Evesham, Pershore and Westminster, were lords of seven-twelfths of Worcestershire, that the church of Worcester was lord of one quarter of that shire and lord of the triple hundred of Oswaldslaw. How did that church become the owner of a quarter of a county, to say nothing of lands in other shires? We ought to be able to answer this question in general terms, for among the charters that have come down to us there is no series which is longer, there is hardly a long series which is of better repute, than the line of the land-books which belonged to the church of Worcester. They come to us for the more part in the form of a cartulary compiled not long after the Conquest by the monk Heming at the instance of Bishop Wulfstan.

Now the answer that they give to our question is this:—With but few exceptions, the donors of these lands were kings or under-kings, kings or under-kings of the Mercians, kings of the English, and the gifts were large gifts. . . . But to whichever of our oldest churches we turn, the story that it proclaims in its title-deeds is always the same:—We obtained our lands by means of royal grants; we obtained them not in little pieces, here a few acres and there a few, but in great pieces. Canterbury and Winchester echo the tale that is told by Worcester. . . . Then, to choose one last instance, it is said that already in

679 Osric of the Hwiccas gave to an abbess *centum manentes qui adiacent civitati quae vocatur Hát Bathu.* It is not unlikely that this means that a king newly converted to Christianity disposed by one deed of many square leagues of land, namely, of the hundred of Bath. The kingdom of the Hwiccas was not boundless. If Osric executed a few more charters of this kind he would soon have "booked" it all.

Let us then examine with some care the charters that come to us from the earliest period, a period which shall begin with the year 600 and end with the year 750. From this time we have some forty charters sufficiently genuine for our present purpose. With hardly an exception the grantor is a king or an under-king, while the grantee is a dead saint, a church, a bishop, an abbot, or a body of monks. If the grantee is a layman, the gift is made to him in order that he may found a minster. If this purpose is not expressed, it is to be understood. Thus in 674 or thereabouts Wulfhere king of the Mercians gives five manses to his kinsman Berhtferth as a perpetual inheritance. Berhtferth is to have full power to give them to whom he pleases . . . the king makes the gift "for the love of Almighty God and of his faithful servant St. Peter." In other cases the lay donee is to hold the land "by church right" or "by minster right." Indeed there seems to be no single deed of this period which does not purport upon its face to be in some sort an ecclesiastical act, an act done for the good of the church.

These charters are documents of ecclesiastical origin; they are also documents of foreign origin. The bishops and abbots have brought or have imported models from abroad. The "books" that they induce the kings to sign are full of technical phrases which already have an ancient history. By way of illustration we will notice one point at which there is an instructive resemblance and an instructive contrast. On the Continent a grantor of lands ends his conveyance with a "penal stipulation." If an heir of his controverts the deed, he is to pay a certain sum, and none the less the conveyance is to remain in full force. In England we can not thus stipulate for a pecuniary penalty; the land-book is still so purely an ecclesiastical affair that the punishment of its violator must be left to the church and to God. So instead of stipulating that he shall pay money, we stipulate that he shall be excommunicated and, if impenitent, damned, but we do not forget to add that none the less the conveyance shall remain as valid and effectual as ever. "If anyone," says Eadric of Kent, "shall attempt to go against this gift, let him be separated from all Christianity and the body and blood of Jesus Christ, *manentem hanc donationis chartulam in sua nihilominus firmitate.*" Such words may look somewhat out of place in their new surroundings; but they are part of a venerable formula.

But what is the model to which in the last resort these documents go back? A conveyance by a Roman landowner. He has in the land full and absolute *dominium* and is going to transfer this to another. Let us observe that the recorded motive which prompts a king to set his cross, or rather Christ's cross, to a land-book is a purely personal motive. He wishes to save his soul, he desires pardon for his crimes. Of the welfare of his realm he says nothing; but his soul must be saved. Sometimes he will give land to an under-king or to an ealdorman, for they also have souls and may desire salvation. He is acting as a private landowner might act. Then he uses terms and phrases which belong to the realm of pure private law. He asserts in the most energetic of all the words that the law of the lower empire could provide that he is a landowner and that he is going to transfer landownership. The land in question is *tellus mea* or it is *terra iuris mei*. Then it is the very land itself that he gives, the land of so many manses, "with all the appurtenances, fields, pastures, woods, marshes." It is no mere right over the land that he gives, but the very soil itself.

No doubt then, if we bring to the interpretation of these instruments the ideas of an earlier or of a later time, the ideas of ancient Rome or of modern Europe, we see the king as a landowner conferring on the churches landownership pure and simple. The fact on which our constitutional historians have laid stress, namely, that sometimes (for we must not overstate the case) the king says that the bishops and his great men are consenting to his deed, important though it may be in other contexts, is of little moment here. The king is put before us as the owner of the land conveyed; it is, he says, *terra mea, terra iuris mei.* The rule, if rule it be, that he must not give away his land without the consent of bishops and nobles in no way denies his ownership. However, we are at the moment more concerned with the fact, or seeming fact, that what he gives to the churches is ownership and nothing less.

But if we loyally accept this seeming fact and think it over, to what conclusions shall we not be brought, when we remember how wide were the lands which the churches acquired from the kings, when we think once more how by virtue of royal gifts the church of Worcester acquired a quarter of a county? When these lands were given to the church were they waste lands? It is plain that this was not the common case. Already there were manses, there were arable fields, there were meadows, there were tillers of the soil. One of two conclusions seems to follow. Either the king really did own these large districts, and the tillers of the soil were merely his slaves or *coloni,* who were conveyed along with the soil, or else the clear and emphatic language of the charters sadly needs explanation. Now if we hold by the letter of the charters, if we say that the king really does confer landownership upon the churches, there will be small room left for any landowners in England save the kings, the churches and perhaps a few great nobles. This is a theory which for many reasons we can not adopt; no one can adopt it who is not prepared to believe that Britain was conquered by a handful of chieftains without followers. The only alternative course seems that of saying that many of the land-books even of the earliest period, despite their language, convey not the ownership of land, but (the term must be allowed us) a "superiority" over land and over free men.

Let us for a moment remember that the wording of a modern English conveyance might easily delude a layman or a foreigner. An impecunious earl, we will say, sells his ancient family estate. We look at the deed whereby this sale is perfected. The Earl of A. grants unto *B. C.* and his heirs all the land delineated on a certain map and described in a certain schedule. That in substance is all that the deed tells us. We look at the map, we see a tract of many thousand acres, which, besides a grand mansion, has farm-houses, cottages, perhaps, entire villages upon it. The schedule tells us the names of the fields and of the farm-houses. Like enough no word will hint that any one lives in the houses and cottages, or that any one, save the seller, has any right of any kind in any part of this wide territory. But what is the truth? Perhaps a hundred different men, farmers and cottagers, have rights of different kinds in various portions of the tract. Some have leases, some have "agreements for leases," some hold for terms of years, some hold from year to year, some hold at will. The rights of these tenants stand, as it were, between the purchaser and the land that he has bought. He has bought the benefit, and the burden also, of a large mass of contracts. But of these things his conveyance says nothing. And so again, in the brief charters of the thirteenth century a feoffor will say no more than that he has given *manerium meum de Westona*, as though the manor of Weston were some simple physical object like a black horse, and yet under analysis this *manerium* turns out to be a complex tangle of rights in which many men, free and villein, are concerned.

We will glance for a moment at two transactions which took place near the end of the seventh century. Bede tells how Aethelwealh king of the South Saxons was persuaded to become a Christian by Wulfhere king of the Mercians. The Mercian received the South Saxon as his godson and by way of christening-gift gave him two provinces, namely the Isle of Wight and the territory of the Meanwari in Wessex, perhaps the hundreds of Meon in Hampshire. Then the same Bede tells us that the same Aethelwealh gave to Bishop Wilfrid a land of eighty-seven families, to wit, the promontory of Selsey: he gave it with its fields and its men, among whom were two hundred and fifty male and female slaves. A modern reader will perhaps see here two very different transactions. In the one case he sees "the cession of a province" by one king to another, and possibly he thinks how Queen Victoria ceded Heligoland to her imperial grandson:—the act is an act of public law, a transfer of sovereignty. In the other case he sees a private act, the gift of an estate for pious uses. But Bede and his translator saw little, if any, difference between the two gifts: in each case Bede says "donavit"; the translator in the one case says "forgeaf," in the other "geaf and sealde." Now it will hardly be supposed that the Isle of Wight had no inhabitants who were not the slaves or the *coloni* of the king, and, that being so, we are not bound to suppose that there were no free landowners in the promontory of Selsey. May it not be that what Aethelwealh had to give and gave to Wilfrid was what in our eyes would be far rather political power than private property?

But over the free land of free landowners what rights had the king which he could cede to another king or to a prelate, saying withal that the subject of his gift was land? He had, as we think, rights of two kinds that were thus alienable; we may call them fiscal rights and justiciary rights, though such terms must be somewhat too precise when applied to the vague thought of the seventh and eighth centuries. Of justiciary rights we shall speak below. As to the rights that we call fiscal, we find that the king is entitled to something that he calls *tributum, vectigal,* to something that he calls *pastus, victus,* the king's *feorm;* also there is military service to be done, and the king, when making a gift, may have a word to say about this.

Now it must at once be confessed that the charters of this early period seldom suggest any such confusion between political power and ownership as that which we postulate. Still from time to time hints are given to us that should not be ignored. Thus a Kentish king shortly after the middle of the eighth century gave to the church of Rochester twenty ploughlands, not only "with the fields, woods, meadows, pastures, marshes and waters thereto pertaining," but also "with the *tributum* which was paid thence to the king." Such a phrase would hardly be appropriate if the king were giving land of which he was the absolute owner, land cultivated for him by his slaves.

A little more light is thrown on the matter by the first rude specimens of a clause that is to become common in after times, the clause of immunity. Already in the seventh century Wulfhere of Mercia, having made a gift of five manses, adds: "Let this land remain free to all who have it, from all earthly hardships, known or unknown, except fastness and bridge and the common host." So in 732 a king of Kent says: "And no royal due shall be found in it henceforth, saving such as is common to all church lands in this Kent." Aethelbald of Mercia says: "By my royal power I decree that it be free for ever from all tribute of secular payments, labours and burdens, so that the said land may render service to none but Almighty God and the church." Yet more instructive, if we may rely upon it, is the foundation charter of Evesham Abbey. Aethelweard has given twelve manses: he then says, "I decree that for the future this land be free from all public tribute, purveyance, royal works, military service (*ab omni publico vectigali, a victu, ab expeditione, ab opere regio*) so that all things in that place which are valuable and useful may serve the church of St. Mary, that is to say, the brethren serving [God] there; save this, that if in the island belonging to the said land there shall chance to be an unusual supply of mast, the king may have pasture for fattening one herd of pigs, but beyond this no pasture shall be set out for any prince or potentate." Now in the first place, these charters speak as though military service is due from land:—I (says the king) declare this land to be free from the "fyrd," from the *expeditio*—or—I declare that it is free from all earthly burdens, except military service and the duty of repairing bridge and burh. We are not saying that there is already military tenure, but we do say that already the "fyrd" is conceived as a burden on land, in so much that the phrase "This land is—or is not—to be free of military service" has a meaning. But after all, land never fights: men fight. Of what men then is the king speaking when he says that the land is, or is not, free from the *expeditio?* Not of the donees themselves, for they are bishops and monks and serve in no army but God's. Not of the slaves who are on the land, for they are not "fyrd-worthy." He is speaking of free men who live on the land; he is declaring that when he has, if so modern a term be suffered, "attorned" them to the church, they will still have to serve in warfare, or he is declaring that they will be free even from this duty to the state in order that the land may be the more absolutely at the service of God and His stewards.

Then military service, along with the duty of repairing bridges and fastnesses, belongs to a genus of dues, of which unfortunately we get but a vague description. There are *vectigalia publica, opera regia, onera saecularia,* there is *tributum,* there is *victus.* How much of the information that we get about these matters from later days we may carry back with us to the earliest period it is difficult to say. Apparently the king, the under-king, even the ealdorman, has a certain right of living at the expense of his subjects, of making a progress through the villages and quartering himself, his courtiers, his huntsmen, his dogs and horses upon the folk of the townships, of exacting a "one night's farm" from this village, a "two nights' farm" from that. The men who have to bear these exactions may well be free men and free landowners; still over them the king has certain rights and rights that he can give away. According to our interpretation of the charters, it is often enough such rights as these that the king is giving when he says that he is giving *terram iuris mei.* He declares, it will be observed, that the land is to be free from *vectigalia* and *opera* to which it has heretofore been subject. But does he mean by this to benefit the occupiers of the soil? No, he has no care whatever to relieve them. Bent on saving his soul, his care is that the land shall be wholly devoted to the service of God. As we understand the matter, whatever *vectigalia* and *opera* the king has hitherto exacted from these men the church will now exact. The king has conveyed what he had to convey, a superiority over free landowners.

It is permissible to doubt whether modern historians have fully realized the extent of the rights which the king had over the land of free landowners. In the middle of Ine's laws, which follow each other in no rational order, we suddenly come upon an isolated text, which says this: "For 10 hides 'to foster' 10 vessels of honey, 300 loaves, 12 ambers of Welsh ale, 30 of clear [ale], 2 old [i.e. full grown] oxen or 10 wethers, 10 geese, 20 hens, 10 cheeses, an amber full of butter, 5 salmon, 20 poundsweight of fodder and a hundred eels." The context throws no light upon the sentence; but in truth no sentence in Ine's laws has a context. What is its meaning? We can not but think that this *foster* is the king's *victus*. Once a year from every ten hides he is entitled to this *feorm*. Perhaps it is a "one night's *feorm*"; for it may be enough to support a king of the seventh century and a modest retinue during twenty-four hours. Still it will be no trifling burden upon the land, even if we suppose the hide to have 120 arable acres or thereabouts. Suppose that the king transfers his right over a single hide to some bishop or abbot, the donee will be entitled to receive from that hide a rent which can not be called insignificant. We dare not argue that this law is a general law for the whole of Wessex. It may refer only to some newly settled and allotted districts. There are other hints in these laws of Ine of some large land-settlement, an allotment of land among great men who have become bound to bring under cultivation a district theretofore waste. But it is difficult to dissociate the *foster* of these laws from the *victus* of the charters, and, quite apart from this disputable passage, we have plenty of proof that the king's *victus* was an incumbrance which pressed heavily upon the lands of free landowners. If in England the duty of feeding the king as he journeys through the country developed into a regular tax or rent this would not stand alone. That duty plays a considerable part in the Scandinavian law-books, and in the Denmark of the thirteenth century we may find arrangements which are very like that set forth in Ine's law.

Whatever be the origin of the king's *feorm*—and if we find it in the voluntary gifts which yet barbarous Germans make to their kings, we may none the less have to admit that it has been touched by the influence of the Roman *tributum*—it becomes either a rent or a tax. We may call it the one, or we may call it the other, for so long as the recipient of it is the king, the law of the seventh and eighth centuries will hardly be able to tell which it is. The king begins to give it away: in the hands of his donees, in the hands of the churches, it becomes a rent. This is not all, however, that the king has to give, or that the king does give, when he says that he is giving land. That he may be giving away the profits of justice, that he may be giving jurisdiction itself, we shall argue hereafter. But probably he has even in early days yet other things to give, and at any rate in course of time he discovers that such is the case. He can give the right to take toll, he can give market rights. It is by no means impossible that he has forest rights, some general claim to place uncultivated land under his ban, if he would hunt therein, and some general claim to the nobler kinds of fish. Then again, in the eleventh century we find men owing services to the king which he still receives rather as king than as landlord, and the sporadic distribution of these services seems to show that they are not of modern origin. . . . Every increase in the needs of the state, in the power of the state, gives the king new rights in the land, consolidates his seignory over the land. If a fleet be formed to resist the Danes, the king has something to dispose of, a new immunity for sale. If a geld be levied to buy off the Danes, the king can sell a freedom from this tax, or he can tell the monks of St. Edmundsbury that they may levy the tax from their men and keep it for their own use. This, we argue, is not a new abuse, a phenomenon which first appears in the evil feudal time when men began to confuse *imperium* with *dominium*, kingship with landlordship, office with property, tax with rent. On the contrary, we must begin with confusion. In some of the very earliest land-books that have come down to us what the king really gives, when he says that he is giving land, is far rather his kingly superiority over land and landowners than anything that we dare call ownership.

Not that this is always the case. Very possible is it that from the first the king had villages which were peopled mainly by his theows and læts, and intertribal warfare may have increased their number. But the charters, for all their apparent precision, will not enable us to distinguish between these cases and others in which the villages are full of free landowners and their slaves. The charters are not engendered by the English facts; they are foreign, ecclesiastical, Roman. By such documents, to our thinking, the king gives what he has to give. In one case it may be a full ownership of a village or of some scattered steads; in another it may be a superiority, which when analyzed will turn out to be a right of exacting supplies of provender from the men of the village; in a third, and perhaps a common case, the same village will contain the *mansi serviles* of the king's slaves and the *mansi ingenuiles* of free landowners. He no more thinks of distinguishing by the words of his charter his governmental power over free men and their land from his ownership of his slaves and the land that they are tilling, than his successor of the eleventh or twelfth century will think of making similar distinctions when he bestows a "manor" or an "honour."

We have been suggesting and shall continue to

suggest that at a very early time, a time beyond which our land-books will not carry us, the king is beginning to discover that the whole land which he rules is in a certain and a profitable sense his land. He can give it away; he can barter it in exchange for spiritual benefits, and this he can do without wronging the free landholders who are in possession of that land, for what he really gives is the dues (it is too early to say the "service") that they have owed to him and will henceforth owe to his donee. . . . The beef and the cheese and the Welsh ale that he might have levied from a district he invests, if we may so speak, in what he is being taught to regard as the safest and most profitable of all securities. He obtains not only remission of his sins, but also the friendship and aid of bishops and clergy. And so large stretches of land are "booked" to the churches. It is to be feared that if the England of the sixth century had been visited by modern Englishmen, the Saxon chieftains would have been awakened to a consciousness of their "booking" powers by offers of gin and rifles.

We must wait for a later age before we shall find the kings freely booking lands to their thegns without any allusion to ecclesiastical purposes. Indeed it may be said that the Anglo-Saxon land-book never ceases to be an ecclesiastical instrument. True that in the tenth century the kings are booking lands to their thegns with great liberality; true also that there is no longer any pretence that the land so booked will go to endow a church; but let us observe these books and let us not ignore the recitals that they contain. Why does the king make these grants? He says that it is because he hopes for an eternal reward in the everlasting mansions. This has perhaps become an empty phrase: but it has a history. Also it is needed in order to make the deed a logical whole. Let us observe the sequence of the clauses:— "Whereas the fashion of this world passeth away but the joys of heaven are eternal; therefore I give land to my thegn so that he may enjoy it during his life and leave it on his death to whomsoever he pleases, and if any one shall come against this charter may he perish for ever; I have confirmed this gift with the sign of Christ's holy cross." Some piety in the harangue (*arenga*) is necessary in order to lead up to the anathema and the cross; it justifies the intervention of the bishops, who also will make crosses and thereby will be denouncing the church's ban against any one who violates the charter. And who, we may ask, is likely to violate the charter? The donee's kinsfolk may be tempted to do this if the donee makes use of that testamentary power which has been granted to him (as, for instance, by leaving the land to a church) more especially because it may be very doubtful whether in impeaching such a testament they will not have the folk-law on their side. Such in brief outline is—so we think—the history of book-land. It is land (or rather in many cases a superiority) held by royal privilege under the sanction of the anathema.

VII

Ownership in Old English Communities

Published in 1898, Township and Borough *contains a series of lectures delivered by Maitland at Oxford in the preceding year. In the extracts selected here Maitland enlarges upon the need of freeing the mind from bondage to modern conceptions and legal distinctions if one hopes to understand the vague and hazy ideas in the minds of those who dwelt in old English villages and boroughs: "We shall have to think away distinctions which seem to us as clear as the sunshine; we must think ourselves back into a twilight."*

. . . A student of our towns and villages must come to close quarters with some legal ideas, and the task of unravelling their history is not going to be so easy as it looked a while ago. That is a warning which comes to us from many quarters. We may see it in Mr Baden-Powell's book on the Indian Village, and in Dr Gierke's book on the German Community. We may see it everywhere. We shall have to think away distinctions which seem to us as clear as the sunshine; we must think ourselves back into a twilight. This we must do, not in a haphazard fashion, but of set purpose, knowing what we are doing.

. . . Before we have gone far back in our own history, the "belongs" (if I may so say) of private law begins to blend with the "belongs" of public law; ownership blends with lordship, rulership, sovereignty in the vague medieval *dominium*, and the vague medieval *communitas* seems to swallow up both the corporation and the group of co-owners. We know or are beginning to know this; but a particular example may bring it sharply before our minds. When King John granted the vill of Cambridge to the burgesses and their heirs, did he mean to confer an ownership of the soil upon a municipal corporation? One point seems certain. Neither John nor his chancellor would have understood the terms of our question. Both the right that is given and the person or persons to whom it is given are hazily and feebly conceived.

You know why I say "person or persons." I think that the historian of our towns will have to face that difficulty. Also I fancy that in this country lawyers have done something to deter historians from fairly facing it, by concealing from them its moral and economic interest. The invention of "fictitious personality," as it is sometimes called, is put before us as a feat of skill, an ingenious artifice of jurisprudence. The inference is readily drawn that it concerns only lawyers. But is that true?

In 1833 Cambridge, like other boroughs, was visited by royal commissioners. Of Cambridge, as of most other boroughs, they reported some evil tidings. In Cambridge, however, they found what was rare, a member of the corporation who courageously defended what they regarded as a bad abuse: namely, the sale of some pieces of the corporation's land to corporators at small prices. "He thought" we are told "that the property [of the corporation] belonged *bona fide* to the corporation and that they had a right to do what they pleased with their own." "Such," the commissioners exclaim, "is the theory of a member of the Cambridge common council, which, however frequently it may have been acted upon, has seldom, we conceive, been openly supported by so unflinching an advocate."

And yet the common-councillor's theory seems verbally plausible. The property of a corporation is unquestionably its property, and are we to be angry whenever a noun in the singular governs a verb in the plural? If so, we had better not read medieval records, for even *universitas* is sometimes treated as a "noun of multitude."

I must not carry further the defense of my fellow-townsman. Certainly in this context there is a vast difference between "its" and "theirs." In our eyes this is a difference between decency and scandal. But I think we have reason to believe that it is also a difference between modernity and antiquity, and (if I may so use the words) between urbanity and rusticity. The common-councillor was ignoring a moral and economic achievement accomplished in the medieval boroughs, the differentiation of "its" from "ours."

. . . We feel that the disclosures of 1833 were disgraceful. We observe also that few men have had the courage of this common-councillor. Very rarely in the great towns had the property of the corporation been frankly divided among the corporators. Too often it had been sold or let to them at an undervalue. The inadequate price or inadequate rent was a tribute paid to civic virtue. The corporators in the great towns had known and felt that the property of the corporation was not exactly their own *bona fide*.

But it is, so I think, with other feelings that we observe what had happened in some little towns, or rather villages, which long ago received a few chartered privileges from a medieval baron and therefore were allowed a precarious place on the roll of English boroughs. Economically they were rural villages. In one case we are told that "most of the senior burgesses were in the rank of labourers." Well, there used to be a common pasture; it had disappeared; it had been cut up into plots, which had been let on long and highly beneficial leases to burgesses, or rather villagers. Now I should like to put this to you as a question not of law, but of morals: Has any great wrong been done? Do you feel inclined to speak of misappropriation? For my own part I am not prepared to use very hard words, because I do not expect to find in a village community of an old type any clear perception of a difference between "its" and "theirs," and, if such a perception I found, I should doubt that it was born in the village.

Let us admit then that the corporateness of the old boroughs was not manufactured but grew and is perceptibly older than the charter for Hull. On the other hand, there seems to be some danger in these days that we may misplace and antedate those thoughts and feelings and practices which are the essence of corporateness, and by so doing may turn history inside out.

There are some who would have us believe that groups, families, clans, rather than individual men, were the oldest "units" of law: that there was law for groups long ages before there was law for individuals. In the earliest stage, we are told, all is "collective." Neither crime nor debt, neither property nor marriage nor paternity can be ascribed to the individual. Far rather the group itself, the clan or family, is the one and only subject of rights and duties.

Now I can not help fancying that a laudable reaction against the individualism of Natural Law has carried some of us into extravagant phrases. To me it seems that the supposed law for groups, whenever it becomes concrete and practicable, is found to involve a great deal of law for individuals, and sometimes of law that looks suspiciously modern. Sir Henry Maine has said that "the Family, in fact, was a Corporation." But then, he has also told us that "the Patriarch, for we must not yet call him the Pater-familias," was a "trustee for his children and kindred," and "in the eye of the law" represented the collective body. This patriarchal trustee, who represents a corporation, looks to me, I must confess it, suspiciously modern. He may be a savage, but he is in full evening dress. At any rate, however, he is an individual man; and, if he is treated as trustee and representative, there is law enough for individuals and to spare.

If we speak, we must speak with words; if we think, we must think with thoughts. We are moderns and our words and thoughts can not but be modern. Perhaps, as Mr. Gilbert once suggested, it is too late for us to be early English. Every thought will be too sharp, every word will imply too many contrasts. We must, it is to be feared, use many words and qualify our every statement until we have almost contradicted it. The outcome will not be so graceful, so lucid, as Maine's Ancient Law.

But just in this matter of archaic "corporations," what I think we should demand before we let the phrase pass is some proof that the men who constitute the group are prepared to contrast what Dr

Gierke calls the all of unity with the all of plurality, to contrast an "its" with an "ours," or to say that though this land is ours in a certain sense, it is not ours in another sense, for we are not co-owners of it.

This is the contrast which emerges in the medieval boroughs slowly and painfully. Less help than we might have expected had been given by the example of religious groups, religious houses. For one thing, the group that was in the strictest sense "religious" was too monarchical to be instructive; the abbot's will was the abbey's will. Then again, in the ecclesiastical sphere the dead yet living saint could appear as a person to whom rights and duties and even wrongful acts might be attributed. No such supernatural aid would come to the burgesses in their effort to separate their unity from their plurality. I need not say that there were no joint-stock companies to serve as a model.

The borough community is corporate; the village community is not. Some injustice will be done by every distinction of this sort. Law sees differences of kind where nature has made differences of degree. Some little accident might throw a township on one side of the line or the other. No accurately exhaustive list of our corporate boroughs ever was or could be made. But in rough, so it seems to me, the law was right. The village community was not corporate. Corporateness came of urban life.

If I say a few words about the English village of

the oldest time, they will be said very diffidently: the more diffidently because I feel the temptation to take a side and knowingly yield to it. Admitting that there are in this village both unity and plurality, if I in some sort plead the cause of plurality, this will be because our natural tendency is to overestimate the unity. No sooner have we allowed, as allow, I think, we must, that the land belongs to a community, than our modern brains are at work conferring ownership upon a corporation. The Village, with a capital V, has land. Its land is owned by an "it" whose will is manifested in the votes of an assembly.

I fear that we are instilling into our primitive village thoughts which even in the boroughs of the twelfth century were waiting a speech that would not come.

Now, in the first place, I can not see the English village of the remotest days as populous. I doubt we ought often to suppose more than some ten to fifteen households, and I think it no paradox but a very simple truth that the fewer our numbers, the further we are from any constitutional unity. It is the crowded town that is one: a Town with a capital *T*. When there is no longer any hope of continuous agreement, then comes the demand for and the possibility of an organic union, a permanent habit of agreeing to differ and yet to be permanently one.

Mere numbers are important. I am persuaded that

we hurry the history both of our villages and of our towns because we fill them too full. There are some thoughts which will not come to men who are not tightly packed.

Then it should be remembered that we are tempted or compelled to draw inferences about free villages, from villages that are not free. We see the village of the thirteenth century. We see it in its "extents" and its court rolls, with a good deal of organization. But it is no longer a free, a lordless village. Far otherwise; most of its inhabitants are the lord's bond-men, his *nativi*. By a mental process we remove the lord and set the villeins free. Too often, so it seems to me, we make these changes and suppose that all else will remain unchanged, that the organization, the bye-laws, the court, will remain, though the lord has gone. But does not the village owe much of its compactness to its lord? His hall has become a centre for this little world. If we remove that hall, the village will not be disintegrated, but it will be decentralized.

I am not very hopeful of a portable village community which we might take about with us from one quarter of the globe to another. A Natural History of Institutions is a fascinating ideal, but we must have a care or our Natural History will bear to real history the relation that Natural Law bore to real law. Explorations in foreign climes may often tell us what to look for, but never what to find. If we have to consider the village community as organism, we must consider it also as organ or member of a larger whole. We must not transplant it unless we are prepared to take with it much that is not-itself. That our own village community of the oldest time had no jurisdiction, no power of speaking right, of deeming dooms, must I think be admitted: Dr Stubbs has said as much. Therefore, before we borrow traits from remote lands, the jurisdictional and governmental scheme that prevails there should be examined.

But, to return to our pastures. Are not "the green commons" of the village too common to be owned by a community? Perhaps I put the question ill; but in one form or another it should be put, for popular expositions of the village community will sometimes leave this question in the happy haze of "collective ownership." Now I am very ready to believe that haze is its native atmosphere, and that, when we have plucked it out and inspected it in the modern daylight, we must once more tenderly put it back into the medieval muddle. That seems to me a work which Dr Gierke has been admirably performing in his fascinating book. Only let us know that haze is haze. May be there is an element of co-ownership in the case and an element of corporate ownership. May be our ancestors did not distinguish the all which is plurality from the all which is unity. But we must. If we do not, we ought to applaud the common-councillor who says that the property of a municipal corporation is *bona fide* "their" property.

When in 1835 Parliament took the municipal corporations in hand, it taught them that their revenues were to be expended "for the public benefit of the inhabitants of the towns." The public, not the common, benefit. Had the word *common* been used, might not the inhabitants have divided the income among themselves? But that is the word which haunts us in the middle ages. Even in the boroughs the common bell calls the commons of the town from the common streets and the green commons to the common hall, and in common hall assembled they set their common seal to a lease of their common land, for which a fine is paid into their common chest. All is common; nothing public; the English for *res publica* is commonwealth; the public house was once a common inn. But what is common to us, is it not partly yours and partly mine? We are tempted to think so.

Suppose that we place a pure and unfettered ownership of the pastures in an *universitas* of villagers. Will their idea of community be realized if the pasture rights of the *singuli* are at the mercy of the assembled body? These rights are so necessary to every husbandman that any decisive exhibition of that ownership which we attribute to the *universitas* must go far towards destroying the bond which holds these men together.

I believe that before the Reformation of 1835 there were some boroughs in which the pasture land stood absolutely at the disposal of the municipal corporation. The individual burgess merely because he was a burgess was allowed to turn out beasts upon this land, but he had no right which hampered the power of the corporation to sell the land or put it to some other use. Such right as he had we might compare to the right that the fellow of a college has to sit in the "common" room or play at bowls in the college garden. But you will, I think, find that even in the boroughs this supremacy of the corporate One over the pasture rights of the plural Many marks a late and high and distinctively urban stage of development; and at the present time there are good reasons why a prudent lecturer should not say that such supremacy existed in any particular borough. All that we know of the rural arrangements of medieval England warns us that the fellow's right to play at bowls in the college garden, a right which would disappear if a resolution in favour of new buildings were carried by a majority of one, must not be our model when we think of the hidesman's right to feed his cattle on the "common" land.

Thus the element of unity that there is in the village may soon begin to appear as a mere power of government and regulation, and instead of a proprietary corporation we may find what we call a "local authority," an organ of subordinate government. The transition is easy because the line between public and private law is not drawn, is not felt. Am I putting this clumsily and pedantically? Let me give an example. The pig, which plays a troublesome part in the medieval town, may serve. Now suppose that some town council or parish council forbids me to keep a pig in my back-yard. It no more claims a proprietary right in my back-yard than it claims a proprietary right in my pig. But if a village moot forbids the villagers to put pigs on the common, because pigs rout up the ground, this is a more ambiguous act. We may see in it a proprietary claim, a claim to own the waste and decide what shall be done with it, or merely a claim to that sort of police power which endeavours to prevent harm by ringing pigs and muzzling dogs. Especially if there is a lord pressing forward his right to all that is not definitely appropriated, the old right of the community may take this turn towards a merely regulative power, which in the end may be regarded as delegated by the state.

To us a crucial question would be: What are the powers of a majority? There should apparently be some sphere within which the will of the majority should prevail, and then there should be indefeasible rights. But we have every reason to believe that this question was obscured from view.

One of the great books that remain to be written is The History of the Majority. Our habit of treating the voice of a majority as equivalent to the voice of an all is so deeply engrained that we hardly think that it has a history. But a history it has, and there is fiction there: not fiction if that term implies falsehood or caprice, but a slow extension of old words and old thoughts beyond the old facts. In the earlier middle ages it is unanimity that is wanted; it is unanimity that is chronicled; it is unanimity that is after a sort obtained. A shout is the test, and in form it is the primary test to-day in the House of Commons. But the few should not go on shouting when they know that they are few. If they do, measures can be taken to make them hold their peace. In the end the assembly has but one voice, one audible voice; it is unanimous. The transition to a process which merely counts heads or hands is the slower because in some manner that no arithmetic can express the voices of the older, wiser, more worshipful, more substantial men are the weightiest. The disputed, the double elections that we read of in every quarter, from the papal and imperial downwards, tell a very curious story of constitutional immaturity. But until men will say plainly that a vote carried by a majority of one is for certain purposes every whit as effectual as an unanimous vote, one main contrast between corporate ownership and mere community escapes them.

In an immobile state of society this contrast and many other contrasts may remain latent for a long while. As a test of ownership we are wont to think of alienability. But if the villagers once meditate an alienation of their pasture land the existence of the community is already in jeopardy. As a matter of fact (such is my guess) the ownership of the waste land was in most cases crystallizing round another centre, the lord to whom the village had been "booked" by the king. There was no awkward plurality in him. Between village and borough there is no insuperable gulf, and, if our villages had remained lordless they might perhaps in course of time have exhibited the decisive symptoms of corporate unity; but I imagine that in the old days the community was too automatic to be autonomous, too homogeneous to be highly organized, too deeply immersed in commonness to be clearly corporate, too plural to be legal unit, too few to be one. And at any rate I feel that we shall hardly take an interest of the right kind in the history of our boroughs, unless we are first persuaded that many ideas which are in all our heads and inexpugnable therefrom first came to light and dominance in urban life.

VIII

The Suitors of the County Court

The article which is here reprinted in full, except for the footnotes, was published in the English Historical Review *in July, 1888. It did much to change opinion regarding the composition of the county courts in medieval England. The view that had generally been accepted was that they were normally attended by all the freeholders of the counties. Maitland came to the conclusion, on the contrary, that the county court (at least in its ordinary form, as distinguished from its form on special occasions, as when it was summoned to meet the king's itinerant justices) was an assembly of only those persons who were under obligation to attend because "suit to the county court" was a burden resting specifically on land which they held. The evidence on which he based his opinion came mainly from the Hundred Rolls of 1279, which were compiled from the verdicts of local juries in response to questions put to them by royal commissioners. (An excellent account of the Hundred Rolls is given by Helen M. Cam in her book,* The Hundred and the Hundred Rolls: An Outline of Local Government in Medieval England.) *When the counties were called upon to send representatives to parliaments, these representatives were elected in the county courts.*

Who were the suitors at the county court? The generally accepted answer is, all the freeholders of the county. But as regards the thirteenth century there seems to be a great deal of evidence that this was not so. The opinion which our documents favour is much rather this: that suit to the county court was not an incident of freehold tenure, but had become a burden on specific lands; and that when the number of freeholders was increased by subinfeudation, the number of suitors was not thereby increased. This vill or this manor or this tract of land which belongs to A, owes suit to the county court; A enfeoffs B, C, and D with pieces of land; the whole vill, manor, or tract still owes the accustomed suit, but it owes no more; by whom this suit shall be done is a matter that A, B, C, and D settle among themselves by the terms of the feoffments. In this respect the burden of suit of court is very like the burden of scutage; the amount of scutage is not increased by the creation of new sub-tenancies, but the ultimate incidence of scutage can be settled by feoffor and feoffee.

The Hundred Rolls of 1279 supply a large stock of illustrations, a few of which shall be given. In

Cambridgeshire the greater part of the vill of Bottisham is held of the earl of Gloucester by the priors of Anglesea and Tunbridge; but there are two tenants of the earl's there who do suit to the hundred and county courts for the whole township: *Dominus Simon de Mora tenet unam virgatam terre de eodem Comite et facit sectam ad comitatum et hundredum pro Comite et pro tota villata;* Martin son of Eustace holds two virgates on the same terms. The abbot of Ramsey has a manor at Burwell in the same county; the jurors do not know that he does any service for it except two suits to every county court; *facit duas sectas comitatus Cantebrigie de comitatu in comitatum.* But these two suits are actually done for him by two tenants; J. A. holds a hide and does one suit to the county and to the hundred from month to month for the abbot; B. B. holds ninety acres and does one suit to the county and to the hundred for the abbot. In Croxton in the same county there are two manors; the lord of one does two-thirds of one suit (*duas partes unius secte*) to the hundred and county; the remaining one-third is done by a freehold tenant of the other manor. The suit is thus split into fractions; at Yaxley a tenant owes a half-suit to the county court and an entire suit to the lord's court (*dimidiam sectam, sectam integram*). At Isleham again the suit has been partitioned; for half the year it is done by H. H., for the other half of the year by two tenants of his. Indeed in these rolls it is a quite common thing to find some one of the freehold tenants marked out as doing the suit for the manor or the vill; this is the service or part of the service whereby he "defends" his land against the lord (*defendit duas virgatas terrae faciendo sectam ad comitatum Huntingdonie et ad hundredum de Normancros pro dicto domino*). In Oxfordshire the jurors have a technical name for such a tenant; he is the *attornatus feoffatus.* At Shifford the abbot of Eynsham has a manor for which he must come twice a year to the hundred court, and he owes suit from three weeks to three weeks by (*per*) William Freeman his enfeoffed attorney and his only freehold tenant. The prior of Deerhurst owes one single suit (*debet unicam sectam*) to the county of Oxford for his manor of Taynton, and this is done for him by J. S. his attorney enfeoffed for this purpose in ancient times (*attornatum suum ad hoc antiquitus feoffatum*). Many of the Oxfordshire landowners owe suit to the county court but twice a year.

In the monastic cartularies we find the same thing. Thus, at Hemingford, according to the Ramsey Cartulary, Simon Geoffrey's son holds two virgates for which he "defends" the township at the county and hundred, and when the justices in eyre come round he must appear as reeve (*erit loco prepositi*). At Ellington, John John's son holds a hide for which he does suit to every third county court; at Holywell, Aspelon of Holywell does the suit to the county and hundred, at Broughton it has been done by Nicholas Freeman. We can trace John of Ellington from the cartulary to the hundred roll, and still find him doing his "one-third part of one suit" to county and hundred. Turning to the Gloucester Cartulary, we find a charter of feoffment whereby the feoffee is bound to acquit the vill from suit to all courts of the hundred, or of the county or of justices in eyre, and all other suits which pertain to the said vill. At Clifford, R. E. and another freeholder pay no rent, but are bound to do the lord's suit to the county and hundred; and if by their default the lord be distrained, they must indemnify him. At Northleach is a freeholder who in respect of his land owes suit for the lord to the county court of Gloucestershire and to all the hundred courts of Cirencester, and must remain before the justices in eyre during the whole of their session. A particularly clear case occurs on the Ramsey manor of Cranfield in Bedfordshire: there are four virgates which pay no rent because they defend the whole township from suit to the hundred and county courts—they are virgates *quae sequuntur comitatum et hundredum pro tota villata*; and this is an ancient arrangement, the result of some *vetus feoffamentum*.

All this seems inconsistent with the notion that every freeholder as such owes suit to the county court. The quantum of suit due from the whole county is regarded as having been once for all fixed at some remote time. Very usually a vill is the unit which owes a full suit. In that case the lord of the vill, if the vill is owned by one lord, is primarily liable to do the suit or get the suit done: usually he has stipulated that it shall be done for him by one of his feoffees—the feoffee, let us say, of a particular virgate. Then as regards the feoffor that virgate is burdened with the suit, and the burden will lie on that virgate into whosesoever hands it may come.

Really when one looks at the Hundred Rolls it is quite impossible to suppose that every freeholder did suit to the county. There are too many freeholders for that. On many manors, it is true, there were hardly any freeholders; this is true in particular of the manors belonging to the religious houses; such houses were as a rule very chary of creating freehold tenancies; they kept but two or three freeholders, one of whom had often been enfeoffed for the special purpose of doing the suit due from the whole manor or township. But on the estates of lay lords there were often many small freeholders. Thus at Bottisham the earl of Gloucester seems to have over forty freeholders. Are they bound to go to the county court month by month? No, two of them do the suit for the whole vill. The *plenus comitatus* was not a very large assembly.

As regards suit to the hundred court we have some yet clearer information. The view taken by the jurors from whose verdicts the Hundred Rolls were compiled, very distinctly was that suit was a burden upon particular tenements, and that the subdivision of those tenements by the process of subinfeudation ought not to increase the number of suitors. They complain that the earl of Surrey, who owns the hundred court of Gallow, has not observed this rule. There was, for instance, a tenement in South Creake containing 100 acres; it owed a single suit; it has been divided into forty tenements, and forty suits are exacted. Many other examples are given. A similar complaint goes up from the hundred of Humbleyard. So, again, when the tenement becomes divisible among coheiresses, the number of suitors should not be increased; the burden of the suit should lie on the share of the eldest sister. That this rule has been infringed is matter of complaint in the hundred of North Erpingham. So in the Bingham wapentake of Nottinghamshire there are but twelve tenements which owe suit; their holders have been enfeoffed for the purpose, and there ought to be no other suitors. The wapentake of Rushcliffe in the same county has but six suitors, each owes suit in respect of a particular tract of land.

How could this somewhat capricious distribution of the burden, to which the Hundred Rolls bear witness, have been effected? By way of answer to this question we may suppose—this can be but an hypothesis, for evidence fails us—that when Henry I revived and enforced the duty of attending the local courts, that duty was conceived as being incumbent on all freeholders, or rather (and the exception is important) on all freeholders who or whose overlords had no chartered or prescriptive immunity; but that it was also conceived as being, like the taxes of the time, a burden on the land held by those freeholders, so that when the land held by one of them was split up by subinfeudation or partition among heiresses, the number of suits due was not increased. Some such supposition seems to be warranted by the "Leges Henrici Primi," which after Dr. Liebermann's researches we may ascribe to Henry I's reign. All the *terrarum domini* are bound to attend; but if any lord attends by himself or his steward, he thereby acquits his whole demesne. This last passage may very well mean that if he bestows part of his demesne on a feoffee, a single suit will acquit them both. That during the thirteenth century the number of freeholders increased rapidly, there can be no doubt; but an increase in the number of freeholders did not mean an increase in the number of suits due to the county court.

Of course it may be that on special occasions, in particular to meet the justices in eyre, all the freeholders were bound to attend the county court. But it is possible to doubt even this. The words in the writ of summons directing all freeholders to come may well have been understood to mean all freeholders who owed suit. An examination of the amercements for non-attendance and the "essoins of the general summons" found on the eyre rolls might throw some light upon this problem; to a superficial glance they do not seem nearly adequate to support the received opinion. But at any rate it seems plain that the ordinary form of the county court, the *plenus comitatus* which heard cases and delivered judgments, was not an assembly of all freeholders, but an assembly of those persons who by means of proprietary arrangements between lords and tenants had become bound to do that fixed quantum of suit to which the county court was entitled. It was not an assembly of the king's tenants in chief, though probably the persons primarily liable were in many or most cases the tenants in chief. On the contrary, the person who does the suit, and who is bound by tenure to do the suit, is sometimes a small socager holding a single virgate. But though it was not an assembly of tenants in chief, it was not an assembly of all freeholders.

It is impossible to speak of this matter without perceiving that there is a big question as to "the county franchise" in the near background. That question we need not now attack; but before it is solved we ought to have a clear opinion as to who were the persons bound to do suit at the county court, and it is here humbly submitted that the received opinion as to this obligation does not harmonise with the evidence. Of course, it is conceivable by us that though all freeholders were not bound to attend the court, still all had a right to attend. But would such a right have been conceivable by a man of the thirteenth century? If we asked him as to the existence of such a right, might he not reply by asking us whether those modern Englishmen who are not bound to pay income tax, enjoy the right of paying it if they please? The right to do what nobody wants to do can hardly be said to exist. It would have been very dangerous for any one to attend the county court unless he was bound to go there, for he would have been creating evidence of a duty to attend; *solebat facere sectam, sed modo subtrahit se*—this would have been the neighbours' opinion as to the conduct of an occasional attendant. We mav some day have to confess that the original "county franchise" (if we may use that term to describe what those who had it would have regarded as the very negation of a "franchise"), so far from being settled by the simple rule that all freeholders have votes, was really distributed through an intricate network of private charters and prescriptive liabilities.

IX

In Defense of Bracton and Refutation of Sir Henry Maine

The following extracts are taken from the introduction to Select Passages from the Works of Bracton and Azo, *edited by Maitland for the Selden Society and published in 1895. His purpose was to enable students "to compare the most romanesque portions of Bracton's treatise with the texts from which they are derived." Bracton occasionally referred to the* Corpus Iuris *of Justinian (i.e., the Institutes, the Digest, and the Code), but most of what he knew about Roman law was acquired from the* Summa *of Azo, the Italian jurist who stood at the head of the great school of Roman law at Bologna early in the thirteenth century. Bracton's great treatise is concerned, of course, essentially with English law. His main debt to Roman law, according to Maitland, was in the realm of spirit and method rather than of substance—"not these or those rules, but a method of reasoning about law, of perceiving the interdependence of rules, of making them take their places as members of a body. . . ." Sir Henry Maine's* Ancient Law, *published in 1861, is a work of great repute.*

But here we are to speak only of the Roman, or, as we prefer to call it, romanesque, element in Bracton's work. Now we have been told by Sir Henry Maine, in words that we all remember, that Bracton "put off on his countrymen as a compendium of pure English law a treatise of which the entire form and a third of the contents were directly borrowed from the Corpus Iuris." This is stupendous exaggeration. The amount of matter that Bracton directly borrowed from the Corpus Iuris is not one-third, is not a thirtieth part of his book. The amount of matter that Bracton borrowed from Azo is larger; it may perhaps amount in all to a fifteenth of the treatise. And then as to form, shall we say that a writer who gives some seven folios to the Law of Persons, some ninety to the Law of Things, and near three hundred and fifty to the Law of Actions has directly borrowed the entire form of his book from the Corpus Iuris?

Is it needful, then, to defend him against the charge of intending to deceive? That charge has been made by one whose judgments we cannot ignore, even when we think them wrong. It is thus that Sir Henry Maine wrote of Bracton:—"That an English writer of the time of Henry III. should have been able to put off on his countrymen as a compendium of pure English law a treatise of which the entire form and a third of the contents were directly borrowed from the Corpus Iuris, and that he should have ventured on this experiment in a country where the systematic study of the Roman law was formally proscribed, will always be among the most hopeless enigmas in the history of jurisprudence." Is there really here any hopeless enigma?

If so, let us not spoil the riddle. Had the systematic study of Roman law been formally proscribed in England, Bracton might perhaps have hoped that his project of "putting off" one thing for another would be successful. But unless we give credence to a papal bull that seems no better than a forgery or a joke, or unless we hold that what may not be taught in a school in London may not be taught anywhere within the realm, we have no evidence that the systematic study of Roman law was proscribed formally or otherwise in the England of Bracton's time. And, on the other hand, we have plenty of evidence of the existence in this country of many men who were professional legists, and to whom we must attribute at all events some slight power of recognising a fragment of the Institutes when they saw it. Take for instance William of Kilkenny, keeper of the great seal, who founded exhibitions in the University of Cambridge and sent many a writ to Henry of Bratton; he was, says Matthew Paris, *in iure canonico et civili peritus.*

Was this learned person likely to believe that the *tria praecepta iuris* were first proclaimed by an English justice of assize? Would not speculations about purple patches and painted panels, about islands that arise in mid-stream, seem to him strangely familiar? . . . And if Bracton was rash in hoping that he could impose upon legists such as William of Kilkenny, he must have been even rasher in hoping that he could impose upon his fellow justices—upon Thurkelby or Preston. We need not hesitate before saying that the talk in his book about usufruct (to say nothing of acceptilation) gave the English lawyers of his day just the same little shock that a modern English lawyer would feel if he met with usufruct (to say nothing of acceptilation) in a text-book or a judgment. These are not words that are found upon the plea-rolls. Bracton has two languages: the language of English law and the language of "general jurisprudence." We can even now see when he passes from one to the other, but the transition must have been yet more easily visible to the justices of his own day. Of a truth, then, he was a bold man and "ventured" far.

The limit of his courage we have not yet seen. While engaged in his work of "putting off," he expressly and audaciously refers his readers to the Summa and the Institutes, knowing, of course, that they will not be at pains to look at these books and see how much has been "put off" upon them. Such hardihood is sublime. But when we have once stated our enigma in all its hopelessness, we cannot hope to make even an enigma of it. There has been no "putting off." There has been no "venturing"—at all events, on Bracton's part. No doubt, according to the ideas of our own age, he has treated Azo shabbily. He has treated Glanvill in the same way. He, in his turn, will be similarly treated by the writers of those books that we call "Fleta" and "Britton." But he did no wrong. A literary communism prevailed. There was no property in ideas or in sayings. Otherwise it might be at Bologna, where already there was strenuous competition for students and their fees. Here in England there was no such struggle, and therefore there was no legal or moral copyright in a law-book. The case of the historians is the same. They never think of telling us the names of those whose annuals they appropriate, and yet we do not accuse Florence and Hoveden, Wendover and Paris, of "putting off" or "venturing."

But, it may be said, the gist of the indictment or the enigma is, not that Bracton has stolen another man's work, but that he has represented Roman law to be English law. If so, let us in the first place abandon all talk about "putting off" and "venturing." and in the second place admit that Bracton is only doing what plenty of other people have done, are doing, and will do in many parts of Europe. For example, he is doing what almost at the same moment Pierre de Fontaines is doing in the Vermandois. He is assuming that Roman law may be and ought to be used as subsidiary or suppletory law to fill the gaps in national or provincial custom.

X

The Mirror of Justices

What follows has been taken from Maitland's introduction to The Mirror of Justices, *a volume of the Selden Society's publications edited by William Joseph Whittaker which appeared in 1894. Only one medieval manuscript of the* Mirror *is known to exist, and from this in later times copies were made before a defective printed version appeared in 1642. The unique medieval manuscript was once, so it seems, in the possession of one Andrew Horn, who died in 1328. He was a fishmonger, chamberlain of London, and collector of charters and other kinds of legal documents—"a learned archivist and antiquarian," Maitland suggests. Horn's name appears on the document, with some Latin lines of dubious meaning, but its authorship remains unknown. In an article on this subject by the legal historian I. S. Leadam, entitled "The Authorship of the Mirror of Justices"* (Law Quarterly Review, *XIII, 1897), the opinion is expressed that the book was probably a joint product of two members of Andrew*

Horn's family and transcribed under his direction. How a book in which Edward II is mentioned could have been written during the reign of Edward I might seem to pass all understanding, but it will be noted that this did not baffle Maitland.

In the sixteenth century when the printing press was at work and the manuscript treasures of the monasteries were passing from hand to hand, English lawyers began to turn back their eyes to the old days when our law was first taking a definite shape. The names and the books of Glanvill and Bracton, of Britton and Hengham became current once more. Along with weightier matters there had floated down the stream of time an enigmatical treatise, *The Mirror of Justices.* The first tidings that we get of it are given us by Plowden in his report of a case that was argued before the Exchequer Chamber in the year 1550. He represents Bradshaw, the king's attorney, as contending for the rule *Testis unus testis nullus,* which may be deduced from the book of Deuteronomy; and (said Bradshaw) in ancient times the law of this realm was similar, as is expressed in the book called the *Mirror of Justices,* which was made before the Conquest. The learned attorney had perhaps but cast his eyes upon the book that he thus cited; a careful examination of it he cannot have made. However, from this time forward we begin to see that manuscript copies of the book are being handed about among lawyers.

Coke obtained one, and, as his habit was, devoured its contents with uncritical voracity. "I have," he said, "a very ancient and learned treatise of the laws and usages of this kingdom whereby the commonwealth of our nation was governed about eleven hundred years past."

However, though Coke believed that he had acquired a treatise which set forth the law of King Arthur's day, he did not think that it was written in that very distant age, and he explained away the words by which Bradshaw seemed to have given it a date on the other side of the Norman Conquest. A very slight inspection of it was sufficient to show that it could not as a whole have been compiled before the reign of Edward I. Nothing daunted, the credulous Coke filled his Institutes with tales from the *Mirror*, and, for example, believed that he had a precedent of an appeal of treason which came from the days of King Edmund and in which the appellor's name was Rocelyn and the appellee's was Waligrot. His final opinion seems to have been that the book was written for the more part before the Conquest, but that many things were added to it by one Horn, a learned and discreet man who flourished in the reign of Edward I.

It would be long to tell how much harm was thus done to the sober study of English legal history. The Pseudo-Ingulf himself has hardly done worse. Gradually suspicions collected. It became known that the *Mirror* was to be used with some circumspection, . . . though it is "a very curious specimen of the apocrypha of the law," said Sir Francis Palgrave, "we are compelled to reject it as evidence concerning the early jurisprudence of Anglo-Saxon England."

Meanwhile it had been put into print. This happened in 1642 [the year in which the Civil War began], a marvellously appropriate date for the appearance of a book which proclaimed as the first and sovereign "abuse" that the king is beyond the law to which he ought to be subject. The title page of the printed book bears the words "La Somme appelle Mirroir des Justices vel Speculum Iusticiariorum, factum per Andream Horne." No editor is named, but a Latin note tells us in effect that the text used was a transcript belonging to one Jecell (no doubt the antiquary Thomas Jekyll, who died in 1653), which had been copied from a transcript belonging to Francis Tate (another well-known antiquary) but collated with the ancient manuscript then lying in Benet (now Corpus Christi) College at Cambridge. In 1646 there appeared an English translation by W[illiam] H[ughes], which was republished in 1768 and again in 1840. In 1776 Houard included in his *Traités sur les Coutumes Anglo-Normandes* the first four of the five sections into which the book is divided; the fifth he rejected as being in his opinion a supplement added to the original work by a later hand. It is plain enough that this industrious Norman lawyer, who did much for which we ought to be grateful in publishing our English law-books to the continental world, had no text of the *Mirror* but the poor printed text of 1642, and, as he shows by his conjectural emendations, he was painfully aware of its imperfection. This indeed was known to W. H. in 1646, for he says "And although that the Manuscript Copy be in the Originall very imperfect: the French impression" [that of 1642] is "by misjoining of words in many places without sence, and false printed."

Several seventeenth century copies of the book, including in all probability those that were used in 1642, still exist; but Mr. Whittaker has satisfied himself that they are all derived immediately or mediately from the Corpus manuscript, and that seems to be the one and only medieval manuscript of the *Mirror*.

Our book has long been connected with the name of Andrew Horn, and therefore of Andrew Horn, fishmonger of Bridge Street and Chamberlain of the City of London, we must say a few words. Early in the reign of Edward I. there was a John Horn alderman of Bridge Ward, who served the City now as sheriff now as coroner. Andrew may have been his son, and, if so, came of a good civic family. Late in the fourteenth century we again hear of a John Horn who is fishmonger and alderman. Already in 1305 Andrew was married, for in that year was born to him a son, who, however, lived for but twelve weeks. Andrew himself died in 1328, and we may guess from his will that he left neither wife nor child, for his property was to be divided between his brother William Horn, rector of the church of Rotherhithe, William and Simon Doggett his nephews, and Christina his niece. His executors were his brother William, John atte Vyne and Master John of London, a notary. Already we hear of Andrew in 1308, when along with Richard Horn, Stephen Horn, and other fishmongers, he was sworn to scrutinise the fishmongers' baskets, and one of his own baskets was found deficient in capacity. In 1315 he passed scatheless through a similar ordeal. In 1320 he became Chamberlain of the City, and this post he filled until his death in 1328; but so early as 1311 he had been collecting statutes, charters, and other documents, and having them transcribed for him.

A blunder in the edition of 1642 has hitherto concealed from view the cardinal words of the book. It is thus that the author introduces himself to his readers:—"I, the prosecutor of false judges, and by their procurement falsely imprisoned, searched out the privileges of the king and the old rolls of his treasury wherewith my friends solaced me during my sojourn." He wishes us to believe that he has been thrown into prison by the false judges whose unrelenting enemy he is, and that while in gaol he studied charters and documents and compiled his book.

Is this tale true? Perhaps it may be; but let us

remember that a similar tale stands at the beginning of another law-book coeval with the *Mirror*. The book that we call *Fleta* purports to have been written in the Fleet Gaol. Some have suggested that it was written by one of the justices whom Edward I. imprisoned in 1289. The thought may cross our minds that the *Mirror* is a rival book; but these two tales of imprisoned text-writers do not corroborate each other. On the contrary, they cannot but raise a suspicion that, at least in one of the two cases, the author's incarceration is a "common form," a literary device which will awaken interest and sympathy. At any rate we can see that a man who is going to pose as the prosecutor or sworn foe of false judges has a good deal to gain by pretending that he was imprisoned by their procurement, even though his sojourn in gaol was of that easy and improbable kind that was solaced by a perusal of the rolls of the king's court, to say nothing of the Old and New Testaments "and the canon and the written law." But whether the story be true or false, it is here that the author strikes the keynote of his book. He is, or wishes to be taken for, an enemy of false judges, who himself has suffered by their misdeeds.

One other resemblance there is between the *Mirror* and *Fleta*. Both of them were failures; of each we have only one manuscript. On the other hand, the treatises of Glanvill, Bracton, and Britton were exceedingly successful; they are represented by numerous copies. Even of Bracton's lengthy book at least some forty costly examples have come down to us. The *Mirror* was not taken very seriously by those who lived when it was written.

When was it written? The common answer to this question is that the whole of it cannot have been compiled before the reign of Edward II. Now in some sense or another this statement must be true, for undoubtedly Edward II. is mentioned in this book. But who is this Edward II.? Is he the king who came to the throne in the year 1307? We ought to ask these questions, for we ought to remember that the king who came to the throne in 1272 did not call himself Edward I. In official documents he was simply King Edward, and when he was dead such documents were wont to call him "King Edward son of King Henry," thus distinguishing him from King Edward son of King Edward. Again, when two Edwards had been immediately followed by a third, and it was necessary to number them, men were careful to fix the moment at which the enumeration was to begin: the reigning king was "Edwardus *post Conquestum* tertius." As to Edward fitz Henry, his contemporaries might call him the first or the second or the third or the fourth, according to the extent of their historical knowledge. Few, perhaps, would remember Edward the Elder or Edward the Martyr, but all men had heard of Saint Edward. [Saint Edward was Edward the Confessor.]

What, then, is it that our author tells of "Edward the Second"? This, that until his day the punishment of rape was mutilation. This seems to be a plain reference to a chapter in the Statute of 1285, which made rape a capital crime—a chapter against which the compiler of the *Mirror* has, as we see from other passages, a special grudge. And it is not unlikely that he will call our Edward the First "Edward the Second." He knows Saint Edward, but nowhere shows any acquaintance with Edward son of Alfred or Edward son of Edgar.

We must find better arguments. Now, our author ends his work with a criticism of statutes which are brought under review in an order that is nearly chronological. He comments on Magna Carta, on the Statutes of Merton (1236), Marlborough (1267), Westminster the First (1275), Gloucester (1278), *De Viris Religiosis* (1279), Westminster the Second (1285), Winchester (1285), upon the writ *Circumspecte Agatis*, which is attributed to 1285, and upon the Statute of Merchants, which was made in the same year. The last document he calls a new statute. Here he stops, and I cannot find any allusion to a later statute. Now, unfortunately for us, the age of grand legislation is nearly over by the end of 1285. Still from 1290 we have the famous *Quia Emptores*, which our author would have regarded as a sovereign abuse; from 1295 we have the *De frangentibus prisonam*, which he ought to have mentioned had he known of it, while the *Confirma-*

tio Cartarum of 1297 with its new clauses, and the *Articuli super Cartas* of 1300, would have afforded him abundant materials for criticism and cavil. On the whole, it seems to me that if this book had been newly put into our hands and we had never heard of Andrew Horn, we should have said that it was written very soon after 1285, and probably before 1290. And here it may be noted that if we attribute it to this time we attribute it to the only, or almost the only, time in English history when a sweeping denunciation of the king's justices as perjurers, murderers and thieves would have had enough truth in it to be plausible and popular. This is the time of our one great judicial scandal, for though the justices and clerks who suffered in 1289 may not have been worse men than were some of their predecessors and successors, the exposure of judicial iniquities on a large scale is a unique event. Also we shall see hereafter that the political ideals of our author were such as were becoming antiquated even in Edward I.'s day. However, we must once more repeat that we have before us a man who is quite capable of deliberately mystifying his readers.

For arguments to prove that the *Mirror* was not compiled in the days before the Conquest there can be no need at the present time. But, further, it does not look in the least like an old treatise that has been re-edited by a more modern hand. To those who are learned in the history of the French language, more especially of that dialect of it which was current in England, we must leave all criticism of words and grammatical forms; but any traits that would point to a time before Edward I.s reign have been sought in vain. Express references to his statutes are found in all parts of the book, while almost every sentence in it, though Cnut or Alfred or Arthur may be mentioned, has its point in the thirteenth century and in no earlier age. In particular we must decisively reject the theory that the last section of the work—that which deals with "abuses" —has been tacked on by an editor or continuator to the end of a previously existing book. We have been carefully prepared by the author himself for this last section. His plan is to lay down in one of the earlier sections some doctrine which, as he knows full well, is not the doctrine of King Edward's court, and then to state in the last section that the prevailing doctrine is an abuse, or that Alfred hanged a judge for maintaining it. From first to last he is making an attack on "false judges."

If he knew anything at all about the law of the Anglo-Saxon or of the Norman time, he has studiously kept his knowledge to himself. This is one of the difficulties which meet us if we try to identify him with Andrew Horn, who before the end of his life had at his command the law-books of the twelfth century and a Latin version of the Anglo-Saxon dooms. I do not think that the *Mirror* contains one sentence that has been taken at first hand from the so-called Leges Edwardi Confessoris, Leges Willelmi, or Leges Henrici, to say nothing of the laws of Cnut or of his predecessors. What is more, if we consider the would-be antiquarianism of this book, we must pronounce it to be marvellously innocent, not only of real historical research, but of traditional legendary learning. We have nothing of Brutus, nor of the metropolitan relation which Troy bears to London; not much of Arthur; nothing of Edgar; nothing of the tripartite division of England between Danish, Mercian, and West Saxon law. Saint Edward is not made the hero of the tale; the Norman Conqueror shows no preference for the Danelaw: indeed, the Norman Conqueror is never named. Our author's hand is free, and he is quite able to do his own lying for himself, without any aid from Geoffrey of Monmouth or any other liar. He will not merely invent laws, but he will invent legislators also; for who else has told us of the statutes of Thurmod and Leuthfred?

The right to lie he exercises unblushingly. Now and again we may see traces of some little circumspection. A good instance is given us by the daring fable about the forty-four false judges whom Alfred hanged in the space of a year. He is going to know the names of these judges, and he thinks that he had better not give them the names current in the England of his own day. Henry, John, Richard, Robert, Ralph, Roger will not do. So let them be Watling, Billing, Bermond, and so forth. Watling Street, Billing's Gate, and Bermond's-eye give him useful suggestions. Botolph, Cuthbert, Dunstan, Cede seem pretty safe to a man who goes to church. There is no one to tell him that he had better keep clear of Scandinavian names (and somehow or another he has collected a good many of them), or that Yve and Tristram and Talebot look a little too French or romantic. And then as to the names of the towns whose suitors are to be sent to the gallows, he chooses Dorchester, Cirencester, and Ancaster. If names ending in *chester* are not old, what names are? Let us remember among the exploits of Alfred that he hanged Horn—"Horn michi cognomen." But even the rudimentary caution that we see in this choice of names is rare. Our author knows nothing and dreams nothing of a time before feudalism and knights' fees, of a time when as yet trial by jury had not been invented. If he has heard or read of ancient law, of thegns and ceorls, of *bót* and *wer* and *wíte*, of *griđ* and *mund*, he leaves all this outside his story.

Unless fortune has served him or us very ill, we must hold that he did not scruple to invent tales about times much later than those of Alfred. He ascribes a good deal of legislation to Henry I., Henry II., Richard, John, and Henry III. Some of the tales that he tells of them are not obvious anachronisms; but this general rule holds good, that he says what others have not said and does not say what others have said. For laws of Henry I. (and of Henry I.'s name he is very fond) he does not go to

Henry of Huntingdon, nor to William of Malmesbury, nor even to the Leges Henrici; for laws of Henry II. he does not go to the Gesta, nor to Hoveden, nor to Diceto, nor to Glanvill's book. He does not go to Glanvill's book even when he is going to speak of Glanvill. He is not corroborated; he scorns corroboration.

If now we ask for his motives, we had better for a while use the word *motive* in the sense that Richard Wagner has made familiar. No other law-book is so like "the art-work of the future." It is constructed out of a few leading motives, each of which is frequently reintroduced in some new key with more or less ornament and embroidery. We might pick these out and label them as "the false judge motive," "the Hebraic *talion* motive," and so forth; but any reader will soon see that he can do this for himself, and will find the task amusing. Only of a few main themes shall we here speak.

A strong religious strain runs through his work; indeed, the whole book might be marked *Religioso*. Of course in a medieval law-book, albeit a book of temporal law, we expect to see courteous words about Holy Church and her jurisdiction, even though some of the extreme claims of the ecclesiastical courts are being strenuously resisted. Nor are we surprised when Bracton in fervent phrases preaches a sermon against the corrupt judge and threatens him with everlasting torments. We have something very different in the *Mirror*, something that we shall hardly find elsewhere, least of all in ecclesiastical law-books, for we shall not go far wrong if we call it Puritanism. There is a curious trait of bibliolatry, a tendency to collect precedents out of the Old Testament and to find legal maxims in the ancient laws of the Hebrews, a tendency which the medieval Church very wisely repressed, for it leads to a justification of the judicial combat by the precedent of *David* v. *Goliath* and an acceptation of "Eye for eye and tooth for tooth." But, further, our author chooses to regard every breach of the law as sin. It is of sin that he will write even though this brings him to the flagrant absurdity of a classification of sins as "real, personal, and mixed." Religion, morality, law, these are for him all one; they are for him law. He knows nothing of the distinction, which any canonist would have taught him, between the *forum externum* and the *forum internum*. Hence his enormous and intolerable extension of the boundaries of larceny and perjury. Whatever is morally as bad as theft is theft, and should be treated as such. Hence also the freedom with which he can give the name of law to some rule directly contrary to that which King Edward's courts are enforcing. What I think right is right; what is right is law; any divergence from the rule of right is an "abuse" of the law, even though courts and legislators may be guilty of it.

Let it not be supposed that this obtrusive religiosity is a common feature of medieval law-books.

It is nothing of the kind; it is a very distinctive feature of this book. No doubt in sound and practical treatises we may find religious reflexions, references to Holy Writ, and now and again some fragments of dogmatic theology. But it was no more the fashion in the middle ages than it is the fashion nowadays for a lawyer or for anyone else to speak habitually as if law and law-courts and parliaments existed for the purpose of saving the souls of sinners. Not every book is typical of the age in which it was produced. Every age has had its prophets, its eccentrics, and its paradoxers.

Now the Puritanism, the edificatory design, the unctuous language, may be unaffected. On the other hand, all this may be cant; or, again, it may be a convenient artistic drapery. By assuming the garb of the preacher, and boasting his familiarity with inspired books, this writer may be forging a title to lay down for law whatever rules he would like to enforce, and to tell tales that are not easily credible. So let us be upon our guard.

Then we may see a tendency to dabble in the Canon Law, and yet may be sure that our author is not an instructed canonist.

But, to return from a digression, we shall not easily believe that our author is an expert in the law of the Church. Had he been this, he would assuredly have shown us his hand by some scientific citation. . . . But of the strict scholastic method, the laborious logic that he would have learnt in a school of canon law, there is no trace. Here, as elsewhere, we see the amateur. He has caught hold of some doctrines of *infamia* and of "notoriety," and of the various kinds of ignorance which Bracton had wisely left on one side. He would like to be taken for a well-read decretist; but really his canonical lore seems to be of the kind that an outsider would pick up pretty easily if he haunted the consistories and now and then glanced at a handbook. The confusion between "capital crimes" and "mortal sins," the talk of "mortal actions" and "venial actions," of "real, personal, and mixed sins," the attempt to force upon our temporal law the distinction between "notoriety in fact," and "notoriety in law," the attempt to represent the suitors in the local courts as "judges ordinary": all this, if it be not a display of mere ineptitude, is a display of a perverse originality which amuses itself by playing havoc among technical terms.

So with his Roman Law. Almost all the Romanesque tracks in his book, and they are many, lead us in the first instance to Bracton, with whose work he certainly was familiar. Indeed, but one passage has caught my eye in which he distinctly betrays a knowledge of a Roman text that he could not have obtained from Bracton. This is the definition of theft. . . . But of any study of the Roman books we can see no evidence, while it is almost incredible that he had ever been through a school of professional legists.

And yet he is the man who writes what may in one sense be called the most Romanistic passage that is to be found in any English book. Not only as a matter of general theory does he attribute force to "the written law" and place the Emperor on a level with the Pope and above all kings—Bracton, with Azo's work before him, had been careful to exclude imperial pretensions—but he has the sublime impudence to say that a chapter of an English statute, which he particularly dislikes, is void because it has not received the sanction of Pope or Emperor. This doctrine of imperial supremacy he may have heard from a civilian or from a German merchant. Had it gained a foothold in England a "reception" of Roman law would have been imminent. But we have here only a dream, and one that came through the ivory gate. The orthodox English doctrine, among men who cared to have any doctrine at all about so obvious a matter, was that the king of England was within his realm an emperor *vel quasi*.

It seems plain that this man has Bracton at his elbow. There are in his book passages that might have been borrowed from Fleta or from Britton. But I think it clear that he has gone to the fountain-head.

It is difficult to say what English law-books he has or what he has not used, for he borrows nothing without distorting it. His procedure may be illustrated by what he writes about the crime of mayhem. He seems to have Bracton's account of the law before him, but he adorns it by attributing certain dicta to three ancient judges whom he calls Turgis, Senwel, and Billing, Whether this is the same Billing that King Alfred hanged he does not tell us, and the question is unanswerable, for Billing is the creature of his brain. He is borrowing from Bracton, and concealing the enforced loan by romance.

. . . That Bracton's name should nowhere occur in the book (though Bracton's hero, Martin of Pateshull, is mentioned), that is exactly what we might expect. The man who professed to have read records that never existed was the very man to conceal the name of the writer from whom he learnt almost all that he knew.

That he deliberately stated as law what he knew was not law, if by law we mean the settled doctrines of the king's court, will be sufficiently obvious to anyone who knows anything of the plea rolls of the thirteenth century. If at the present day a man wrote a law-book and said in it, "Law forbids that murderers should be hanged; estates tail cannot be barred; bills of exchange are not negotiable instruments," he would be guilty of no extravagance for which a parallel might not be found in the *Mirror*.

. . . But of a lawyerly interest in law we see very few signs. He does not love to argue, as Bracton loves to argue. He takes no delight in a nice case or a moot point. When we do get from him anything that by courtesy could be called a legal argument, it is fantastic or it is puerile, and this we say judging it, not by any standard of our own day, but by the standard set by Glanvill and Bracton, by Britton and Hengham.

His political theory is simple. He is strongly opposed to an unfettered monarchy and to a king who is above the law. But his ideal of the body which is, or ought to be, a check upon the king, is quaint and impracticable.

He shows some curious leanings towards liberty and equality, an intense and a very unmercantile dislike of imprisonment, more especially imprisonment for debt; a tendency to argue that the lord owes just as much to his man as the man owes to his lord; a desire to give the bailiff just the same remedy against the master that the master has against the bailiff. He holds that the villains are being unjustly treated. For all this, however, he is neither demagogue nor socialist. The feudal arrangement of society is for him a sacred, primeval, unalterable arrangement. He does not denounce it as modern or alien. It was established here immediately after "the coming of the English."

With Andrew Horn, fishmonger and citizen, in our minds, we naturally are on the outlook for any phrase which may exalt the City of London or magnify civic privileges or civic pretensions. . . . But, if I am not mistaken, there is only one matter about which the author of the *Mirror* speaks in the municipal key. That is the residence of aliens within the realm. He holds that a foreigner should not be suffered to dwell here for more than forty days without being put in frankpledge.

Again, we can catch no specifically mercantile strain, no enhancement of the law merchant at the expense of the common law. On the contrary, our compiler has a marked hatred for King Edward's "new" mercantile statute. It allows imprisonment for debt. So doing, it infringes the law of nature and the law of God. It must be confessed that if this book comes from a London citizen and a wealthy fishmonger, he has allowed his own private theories and fancies to override the interested opinions and prejudices of the class to which he belongs, or else—for we must take nothing for granted—knows how to perplex his readers.

But we wrong the man if we wish to make him the representative of a class. He stands, for the sake of art or of mystery, outside all classes, and is not going to tell us whether he is hallowed or lay, gentle or simple, free or bond, from town or from country. If one of his "motives" would suggest one inference about such matters, he will be careful to suggest another inference by another motive.

Is not this man a little too disinterested? Have we not a little too much difficulty in assigning the class to which he belongs? Have we not here the disinterestedness of the smart young man who is amusing himself and laughing in his sleeve? Having told us how Nolling was indicted for a sacrifice to

Mahomet, he may be allowed the licence of the artist. The man who about the year 1289 says that there can be no prescription for franchises, and yet that the lord's consent is necessary if a tenant wishes to make a feoffment, is giving his opinion on two burning questions. One he decides against the nobles, the other in their favour. In each case his opinion is that which the statute roll is going to reject. Such a man is a representative, not of the spirit of the age, but of a disinterested spirit, the spirit of contradiction.

Our author would not be angry, he would be pleased, if we called him a "reactionary" or a "retrogressist." Like most of his contemporaries he believes rather in the good old time than in the good time coming, and it is his cue to restore to pristine purity those "usages" of "our holy predecessors" which have been "turned to abuse." But his list of abuses is a strange medley. As to a few of them we may say with some certainty that if King Edward's justices and officers were guilty of the practices that are denounced, they were knowingly breaking the law. That in and about 1289 there were in high place men who were quite capable of knowingly breaking the law we may learn but too easily from sources incomparably more trustworthy than the *Mirror*. But then these few "abuses" are mixed up with many other "abuses" which really are the newer developments of the common law. The man who calls them "abuses" wants (or makes believe that he wants) to see the stream of law flowing backwards.

When we have to deal with some anonymous and impersonal book we gladly catch at any sentence which seems to reveal by chance some little of the author's life, and sometimes, perhaps, we rear too lofty an edifice of conjectural biography upon a very slight foundation. In the present case we are scarcely tempted to any such constructive feat. The indications are too many and too contradictory.

Howbeit, the strain that dominates the whole book is the dislike of the king's officers and their ways. Corrupt are they and become abominable in their doings; there is none that doeth good, no not one. From the chancellor and the false judges downwards, they are all guilty of offences, which, to give them their plain names, are perjury, larceny, and murder. If King Alfred came back among us he would hang such folk by the score. The system of government is as bad as those who administer it. What our author seems to detest most is any rule that puts the king or any of his subordinates outside the ordinary course of common justice. Writs should run against the king himself. The punishments that have been denounced of late against official oppressions are inadequate; those who are guilty of them are simply perjurers and larceners, and should be treated as such. May we not guess that here, if anywhere, our author is really in earnest, and that a good deal of the rest of his book is but a cloud in which he wraps up his dangerous opinions—opinions, I mean, that may bring him into danger? The man who wants to revive the ordeal, the man who holds that the emperor's consent is necessary if rape is to be made a capital crime, can always laugh at you if you take his words literally. May we not dream and tell our dreams?

The dream that the king of old time could be sued in his own court is a dream that is becoming popular. It is becoming an article of faith among those who have complaints against the king for the time being. Here, more definitely than anywhere else, we can connect the *Mirror* with a political programme that many will accept. Again, if we suppose that the book was written about the year 1289, the talk of "false judges," the hints that the chancery and the exchequer are full of perjurers and thieves, are not without point and truth. It was the time of the great scandal, the time of Solomon of Rochester and Thomas Weyland, the time of Adam of Stratton, the time when Edward appointed commissioners to try his judges, and even a Hengham hardly escaped with untarnished fame. Even here, however, our friend is not going to speak out in simple and straightforward words. He will imply and he will allude. He will not talk of Stratton and Weyland; he will talk of Billing and Watling. He will mix up real grievances with fables and falsehoods and views and visions. He will carp at

Edward's reforming statutes, urging now some pedantic trifle and now some flighty fancy. It is the oddest jumble. At one moment we seem to hear the voice of Bentham, when codification is demanded, and at the next moment we are back among inalienable fiefs. All is wrong; yes, all.

What, then, shall we say of this book? and what shall we call its author? Is he lawyer, antiquary, preacher, agitator, pedant, faddist, lunatic, romancer, liar? A little of all, perhaps, but the romancer seems to predominate. He would like that some of his tales should be believed. He hopes, as other romancers have hoped, to edify as well as to amuse his readers. But he is careful not to tell us when he is in earnest and when he is at play. So to do would not merely be an inartistic blunder: it might end in his being taken but too seriously. He is making an attack on powerful persons, on the king's justices and officers. He is hinting that the royal court is a den of thieves. It is well for him that, if called to account for his words, he can say that he was but telling stories of Alfred and Arthur, and ask you whether you cannot see a joke. That is what makes his work so puzzling to us nowadays. We guess that he wanted his readers to believe some things that he said. We can hardly suppose him hoping that they would believe all. We feel sure that in Paradise, or wherever else he may be, he was pleasantly surprised when Coke repeated his fictions as gospel truth, and erudite men spoke of him in the same breath with Glanvill and Bracton. And yet we cannot say with any certainty when he intends to deceive, when to instruct, when to divert. That is just what he wished. He has puzzled us, and will puzzle us until we know much more than we know as yet of the times in which he lived. It is a variegated, tessellated book, this book of his: *Dichtung und Wahrheit*—or shall we adopt Ihering's *Scherz und Ernst in der Jurisprudenz?* But why borrow from Germany? Perhaps (but even of this we cannot be sure) we have his own description of his own work: it is Ivory and Horn.

To elaborate a theory as to the origin of such a book would be hazardous; but we have seen how two lines of investigation seem to converge. In order to discover the date of its composition we ask what statutes are and what are not, noticed in it, and we are thus led to the years between 1285 and 1290. Then we see that its main and ever-recurring theme is a denunciation of "false judges," and we call to mind the shameful events of 1289. The truth was bad enough; no doubt it was made far worse by suspicions and rumours. Wherever Englishmen met they were talking of "false judges" and the punishment that awaited them. All confidence in the official oracles of the law had vanished. Any man's word about the law might be believed if he spoke in the tones of a prophet or apostle. Was not there an opening here for a fanciful young man ambitious of literary fame? Was not this an occasion for a squib, a skit, a "topical" medley, a "variety entertainment," blended of truth and falsehood, in which Bracton's staid jurisprudence should be mingled with freaks and crotchets and myths and marvels, and decorated with queer tags of out-of-the-way learning picked up in the consistories? While the "false judges" were being soundly lashed, and the gallows was being erected within their view, many other classes of men, especially those which were privileged, could be made to feel uncomfortable by attacks on their interests and their cherished beliefs. Then over the whole a solemn veil of religiosity could be thrown, and startled readers might be assured that all that was written in this book was sanctioned by holy writ and "the usages of our holy predecessors." This, no doubt, is guess-work. It is very possible that some reader more learned or more acute than the writer of these lines will discover some serious purpose, some practical scheme of reform, running through the *Mirror;* I have looked for it and have not found it.

XI

The Year Books and Their Origin

Year Books are notes, written in "law French," of cases tried in the king's courts in medieval England. The earliest ones that have come down to us date from the reign of Edward I, and they continued to be compiled until 1535. The printing of Year Books began in the late fifteenth century, shortly after the introduction of printing in England, and many printed editions were issued in the sixteenth and seventeenth centuries. These old "black letter Year Books," as they came to be called, were full of errors and unsatisfactory from any scholarly point of view, though they, and abridgments of them, were used extensively by lawyers. The modern publication of Year Books edited by scholars was begun in the second half of the nineteenth century with books of the reigns of Edward I and Edward III, which appeared in the Rolls Series in twenty volumes from 1863 to 1911. Early in his career as a legal historian Maitland became interested in the Year Books because of their importance for the history of English law, and under his leadership the Selden Society undertook the publication of those of Edward II. The earliest volumes of this series were edited by him, the first published in 1903. (An excellent general account of the Year Books can be found in Percy H. Winfield, The Chief Sources of English Legal History, *chap. VII, section 4.) Maitland's opinion was that the early Year Books were notes taken in court by law students and not official reports, as had generally been supposed. The first group of excerpts given here (pp. 232-242) are from his introduction to* Year Books of Edward II, *Vol. I (Publications of the Selden Society, Vol. XVII); those following (pp. 242-251) are from his introduction to* Year Books of Edward II, *Vol. III (Publications of the Selden Society, Vol. XX).*

Of the Year Books in General

The Selden Society, which was founded "to encourage the study and advance the knowledge of the history of English law," would hardly be doing all that it might for the accomplishment of this purpose if it made no endeavour to redeem the Year Books from that kingdom of darkness in which they are captives, and to hasten the day when they will once more be readable, intelligible and—we do not fear to say it—enjoyable books. The work has been begun, and well begun, by others. Can we not lend a helping hand?

When all has been said that it is fair to say of England's wealth of legal records, the truth remains that the history of English law from the days of Edward I. to the days of Edward VII. must be primarily sought, not in records properly so called, but in reports. To this may be added that in the way of intellectual products medieval England had nothing more purely English to show than its law reports, its Year Books.

The record of litigation, the officially made and officially preserved record, was not—this need scarcely be said—distinctively English. So soon as many men could write, it was natural that the art of writing should be employed for this purpose. Indeed, we cannot without an effort imagine ourselves in an age when a court of law has no written memory of what it has done. Two main objects a roll would serve. In the first place, it would prevent disputes as to what had happened in some still pending cause. Had the defendant appeared? Had the plaintiff pleaded? Such questions might be conclusively answered even though some judges had died and others filled their place. Secondly, when that cause was finished the recorded result would debar the parties and their heirs from reopening a question that had been closed. In England our *exceptio rei iudicatae* becomes a plea that our adversary is "estopped by matter of record." Then, again, what we may regard as a mere by-end may have been prominent in the minds of those who caused our first plea rolls to be penned. All litigation brought profit to the King. The plea roll told his officers of fines and amercements and directed them in their quest for money. Therefore we need not search for reasons why the work that is done by the King's Court should be set in writing. Probably in the last years of Henry II.'s reign, certainly in the early years of Richard I.'s, plea rolls were being officially made and officially preserved.

Whether the advancement of learning or the formulation of the Court's jurisprudence counted for anything in the counsels of those who set the plea rolls agoing must be very doubtful. After a while, however, when such rolls were beginning to accumulate, it must have become evident that there were upon them valuable precedents. On the other hand, it must have become evident that these same rolls would bear enormous masses of dreary "common form" in which no judge, no lawyer, no student of the law would find any profit, since all was trite routine. It is of the very essence of a series of records that it shall omit nothing because it is dull and commonplace. Directly to consult the ever growing bulk of parchment in the hope of finding a legal principle or an applicable precedent was vain. Moreover, it was important that these conclusive records should be so strictly guarded that even the King's justices would not have unrestrained access to them for the purposes of private study.

. . . Whether Henry of Bratton ought to have had

rolls in his possession, whether he ought to have drawn lines upon them and scribbled words in their margins, who shall say? But the work was done, and the outcome was a collection of some two thousand entries, excerpted from rolls which ranged over the first four-and-twenty years of Henry III.'s reign. And then some five hundred cases were cited in a treatise.

When this great exploit had been performed it may have seemed for a while that the plea rolls would afford the raw material for English case law. But that was not the destined line of development. These sacred records were to be under lock and key, and in England we see no officer told off to make extracts and abstracts which shall be more useful to justices and serjeants than the unwieldy originals could be. On the other hand, we see something that is very new, new in England, new in the world: the vernacular report of an oral debate.

Were these reports official? That they were has been very generally believed and very dogmatically stated from the seventeenth century onwards. So far as we can see, however, these dogmatic statements have for their source some cautious words of Edmund Plowden. That great lawyer has told us that he began to study law in the thirtieth year of Henry VIII. (1538-9)—just at the time, that is, when the Year Books, having become intermittent, were finally ceasing to flow—and that he had heard tell how in ancient days there were four reporters paid by the King. Plowden is careful not to pledge his own word.

He gives us some hearsay about "ancient times." We observe that the story which he repeats will be true enough if at any time during the past centuries there were some officially paid reporters. We observe also that the story, whether true or not, is just such as might find currency if in the new age that was opening—those sad years when the light of the common law was flickering—a continuous supply of reporters could no longer be secured.

When many of the Year Books have been edited and many manuscripts have been explored, we shall be better able than we are at present to discuss this question. Meanwhile let us glance at some of the difficulties which should be faced by any one who believes in the official character of our oldest reports. If reporters were appointed by the King, we might expect to find appointments recorded. If reporters were paid by the King, we might expect to find their stipends mentioned on some fiscal roll. It is easy to prove that the King appointed judges and paid them salaries. Again, if the reports were official, we should expect that the originals, or at all events copies of them, would be carefully preserved by officers of the Court, whereas, so far as we are aware, our manuscript Year Books always come to us from private hands. We might contrast the case of the French "Olim," religiously guarded from prying eyes by the Parliament of Paris. Moreover, we should expect that the manuscripts deriving from an official source would be very much like each other, whereas, at least amongst those which belong to Edward II.'s time, there is wonderfully little similarity. From different manuscripts we sometimes obtain of one case two reports so unlike that we can hardly believe that they have been developed by transcription from a common original. At any rate, the lawyers who copied Year Books, or employed professional scribes to copy them, exercised in full measure a right of omitting cases and parts of cases. Furthermore, we see a most remarkable contempt for the non-scientific detail of litigation: especially for proper names. These very often are so violently perverted that we seem to have before us much rather the work of a man who jotted down mere initials in court and afterwards tried to expand them than the work of an official who had the faithful plea rolls under his eye. Also for a very long time any explicit citation of cases by judges or counsel is so rare that we might easily be guilty of an anachronism if we thought that what was wanted was "authority." We may strongly suspect that what was wanted was instruction, and that these books were made by learners for learners, by apprentices for apprentices. Finally, we seem to see everywhere the outcome of private enterprise. Mixed up with the words attributed to judges and counsel we see notes and comments, criticisms and speculations which a writer who speaks of himself as "I" (*jeo*) gives us as his own. If all of these be mere accretions, then we must deal with our manuscripts in an heroic style, cutting and carving right and left in pursuance of a preconceived theory. And if, on the other hand, all or the bulk of these be the work of an officer royally appointed for work of this kind, let us at least perceive how extremely honourable is the duty confided to him by King and Constitution. Not only may he pick and choose the cases that shall be precedents; not only may he sift the *dicta* that should be remembered from those that should be speedily forgotten; but he may frankly criticize and even blame the doings of the King's judges. In the presence of such an officer even a chief justice might feel small.

Howbeit, as early as 1285, an ever memorable step was taken. Some one was endeavouring to report in the vernacular—that is, in French—the oral debates that he heard in court. In 1293 a fairly continuous stream began to flow. This surely is a memorable event. When duly considered it appears as one of the great events in English history. To-day men are reporting at Edinburgh and Dublin, at Boston and San Francisco, at Quebec and Sydney and Cape Town, at Calcutta and Madras. Their pedigree is unbroken and indisputable. It goes back to some nameless lawyers at Westminster to whom a happy thought had come.

What they desired was not a copy of the chilly record, cut and dried, with its concrete particulars concealing the point of law: the record overladen ious of the interesting names of sages, of justices and with the uninteresting names of litigants and obliv-serjeants. What they desired was the debate with the life-blood in it: the twists and turns of advocacy, the quip courteous and the countercheck quarrelsome. They wanted to remember what really fell from Bereford, C. J.: his proverbs, his sarcasms: how he emphasised a rule of law by *Noun Dieu!* or *Par Seint Piere!* They wanted to remember how a clever move of Serjeant Herle drove Serjeant Toudeby into an awkward corner, or how Serjeant Passeley invented a new variation on an old defence: and should such a man's name die if the name of Ruy López is to live?

Now a certain traditional respect for the Year Books may be taken for granted among English lawyers, or at any rate among members of the Selden Society. And yet it may be allowable to doubt whether we realise to the full their unique position in the history of jurisprudence, in the history of civilisation, in the history of mankind. Endeavouring to the best of our ability to take a wide view of human affairs, let us make a few challenges or ask a few questions on behalf of our Year Books.

Are they not the earliest reports, systematic reports, continuous reports, of oral debate? What has the whole world to put by their side? In 1500, in 1400, in 1300, English lawyers were systematically reporting what of interest was said in court. Who else in Europe was trying to do the like—to get down on paper or parchment the shifting argument, the retort, the quip, the expletive? Can we, for example, hear what was really said in the momentous councils of the Church, what was really said at Constance or Basel, as we can hear what was really said at Westminster long years before the beginning of "the conciliar age"? Suppose that our German cousins had law reports like ours, would not these *Jahrbücher* loom mighty big, not merely in the universal history of law, but in *Culturgeschichte*, the history of civilisation and civilising processes?

These Year Books come to us from the middle age, but are not written in Latin: they are written in French. . . . But is not the very rudeness of the French that we find in these legal manuscripts—and rude it looks even when placed beside Gower's French poetry or Bozon's moral tales—a quality which its best judges would not willingly miss? Is it not a guarantee of genuineness? No one has tried to polish and prune, or to make what is written better than what was heard.

Law, however, is the great matter, and without much fear of contradiction we may affirm that, if to the whole mass of materials for the history of law England had nothing to contribute but these Year Books, England's contribution would still be of inestimable value. A stage in the history of jurisprudence is here pictured for us, photographed for us, in minute detail. The parallel stage in the history of Roman law is represented, and can only be represented, by ingenious guesswork: acute and cautious it may be, but it is guesswork still.

No doubt it is a highly technical aspect of the

work of the law that is displayed on the face of these reports. We see jurisprudence as art rather than as science: we see it even as a game of skill. These books written by lawyers for lawyers remind us of those which chess-players study. Herle castles unexpectedly; Toudeby sacrifices a bishop for the attack; Passeley's management of his pawns was a joy to all beholders. This is what interests the reporter, and let it be confessed that we, at this distance of time, cannot share his interest to the full. But to call a law, or a statement of law, or a book of law "highly technical" is surely no condemnation.

But have we not in these ancient reports too much logic and too little life? On the contrary, we should claim on behalf of the Year Books that, when we consider that they were written by medieval lawyers for medieval lawyers, they show us a marvellous deal of the play of those moral and economic forces of which legal logic is the instrument, and often, if we may so say, the reluctant instrument.

Our commendation of the Year Books will not really be qualified by the remark, perhaps needless, that reports must be read in considerable quantities if they are to be appreciated. They cannot be tasted in sips. Placed in the hands of a foreigner or of a beginner, what could be worse material than the last number of the Law Reports? It is of necessity a jumble of odds and ends. The newest dodge of the company promoter for the evasion of the newest statute jostles some piece of hoary erudition. Even so it is in the Year Books. When many are edited as Mr. Pike has edited a few, no student of English history will dare to neglect them. Indeed it will some day seem a wonderful thing that men once thought that they could write the history of medieval England without using the Year Books.

The time has come when something ought to be said of the manuscripts that we have been using for the compilation of this volume and its two predecessors. The tale that has to be told cannot be very brief, and we must add that it cannot be satisfactory. Still in the course of it we may be able to disclose a state of affairs which will not be wholly devoid of interest in the eyes of students of English history. Two or three preliminary remarks may be offered before we approach our manuscripts.

These Year Books are Law Reports; but the term "Law Reports" is apt to imply a good deal that did not exist in the days of Edward II. or for a long time afterwards. For one thing, it is apt to imply the art of printing and the production of a large number of copies which shall differ from each other in no material respect. For another thing, it is apt to imply what we call "publication." The man who wants a book nowadays has not to order a book to be made for him as he would order a coat to be made for him; he buys a ready-made article. That was not the case, or at least it was not the common case, in the Middle Ages. There were indeed men whose business it was to copy books; they would make you a copy to order if you supplied the exemplar, and occasionally copies of some very useful books might be made in the hope that they would attract purchasers; but to our idea of "publication" there was hardly anything that answered. If you had composed a treatise, you might for love or for reward allow some one else to transcribe it; but the transcription would be his business, and he would be very free to deal with your text in any manner that pleased him: to make omissions, additions, improvements, blunders. The copy was to be his, not yours, and copyright there was none.

Secondly, the term "Law Reports" inevitably suggests to us books that are to be cited in court. It is true that our modern reports serve more purposes than one. They have an educational value. Young men will read them in order to learn the law, and older men will read them in order to amplify their knowledge. Still on the whole we might say that to serve as "authority," to be the base of judgments and of "opinions" that should forestall judgments, is in our own time the final cause of the report. Now when we turn to these earliest Year Books this final cause seems to fall far into the background and almost to vanish. If these books themselves prove anything, they prove that they are rarely, if ever, cited by counsel or justices. . . . If the judges of the fourteenth century had allowed counsel to cite reports, then, the art of printing being still in the future, some stringent measures would have been necessary to insure that books were exactly copied. A little acquaintance with the manuscripts that we have been transcribing would be enough to show that the justices could not have treated them in the way in which a modern judge can treat a modern law report. Those manuscripts differ in every conceivable way. Every citation would begin a new dispute.

Why, then, were these books made? The answer we take to be: Because young men wished to learn the law and to become accomplished pleaders. Before we say more of these young men who, to our thinking, are the begetters of the law reports, a few words about their elders may be in place. The group of men that is here set before us as actively developing the law of England is very small. First there are the judges; but it is to be observed that the three justices of the King's Bench (Brabazon, Roubury, and Spigurnel) are doing very little that is treated as reportable. They are trying cases that are of importance to litigants, but not, as a general rule, cases that involve delicate pleading. Broadly speaking, we may say that these reports are "Common Bench Reports," though a few cases before the justices of assize are noted, and there are reports of eyres that have never yet been printed. Then in the Common Bench there are six justices, namely, Bereford, Trikingham, Stanton, Scrope, Benstede and Bourne; but the last two of them are as yet "mute persons," and

Trikingham is but little better. The administration of the law, so far as we see in these books, is mainly the work of three men: the experienced chief justice, Hervey of Stanton and Henry le Scrope. Then there are about twenty-four counsel in practice. So far as we have gone, a list of the lawyers who are named in the reports for a given year will be almost exactly the same as a list of the "narratores" whom the plea rolls will set before us as having levied fines in the same year: in other words—and this is the point of our observation—we have seen no trace of any class of counsel who have a right to be heard in some but not in all cases: in personal but not in real actions. Some lawyers were much busier than others; still it may be said that, with few exceptions, if a man's name appears once in these Year Books, it soon appears pretty often. Lastly, we will notice that it is not unusual to see three or four lawyers on the same side of the same case. In a truly important case near half "the practising bar" may be retained.

Outside this small group of active practitioners, there stand the "apprentices," the learners, and it must occur to us that they had a great deal to learn, and few means of learning it. We may indeed suppose that to a young man of this time the law that the justices and serjeants discussed did not seem quite so technical, quite so arbitrary, as it appears to us. He could see the social and economic import of rules which we are tempted to regard as perverse displays of ingenuity. Still it is plain that a beginner had a great deal to learn: the mechanism, we might call it, of some thirty forms of action. And it is to be observed that the trenchant statutes of Edward I. had certainly not simplified the law. On the contrary, as is abundantly shown by these reports, they were constantly giving rise to new questions. The first courses of that vast structure of interpretation which we know in the shape of Coke's Second Institute were being reared. Another effect of these statutes deserves a word in passing. These apprentices had no text-book that could be relied on, and in particular none that could be relied on for procedure and pleading. Bracton's treatise was becoming antiquated, and neither the book which we call "Britton" nor that which we call "Fleta" had successfully assimilated the new statutory law. If then these learners were to learn, it would have to be by attending the court and listening to what was said. Their progress would assuredly be more rapid if they took notes of what they heard, if they borrowed and copied and discussed each other's notes.

This we believe to have been the origin of the Year Books. They, or rather the earliest of them (for we would not speak of an age that we have not observed), are students' note-books. Only thus can we account for some of those facts which will be given in evidence hereafter. Meanwhile, however, let us follow our hypothesis a little further. Willingness to lend, to borrow, to co-operate, we may take for granted. We are among young Englishmen. Also we are among the founders of those societies, four of which become eminent as "the inns of court." These young men come up to London for term time; there is plenty of good fellowship among them; they club together; perhaps they jointly hire a house. Perhaps they are already devising "moots" or other exercises which are destined to become more and more academic, and, at all events, we may believe that they talk a good deal of "shop." This is the atmosphere in which note-books multiply. When, therefore, we have before us a dozen manuscripts purporting to contain the reports of a single year, we must not be surprised if the relationships between them are intricate in a very high degree. The assumption that every codex is the offspring of one other codex is a natural starting-point if we would draw a pedigree; but in such a case as ours it may well be fallacious. Our case, indeed, is peculiar. The only people who want these reports live in constant intercourse with each other, and it is not at all impossible that all the copies that exist are to be found within one square mile of the earth's surface. A religious house may keep a Glanvill or a Bracton, a volume of statutes and a register of writs; but manuscript Year Books rarely come to us from monastic libraries. If, then, a man wanted to have a copy of his own, he might easily borrow two or three books from two or three friends, and then he could pick and choose what pleased him best, looking now at one book and now at another.

Moreover, if we regard these books as note-books, we have to remember that a lawyer, like any other man, is entitled to put into his note-book all that he wants and to omit therefrom all that he does not want. He may say, "That case is not likely to be useful, and I shall not copy it." He may say, "That report is too long, and, parchment being expensive, I shall curtail it or condense it." To omission, curtailment, condensation, we could raise no objection. But further, we cannot feel sure that the medieval lawyer did not consider himself entitled to expand as well as to condense: to say "This bit of argument is very ill put, and I can improve it," or "A material fact is missing in this report, and I think that I can supply it by conjecture," or "Really this case wants rewriting from beginning to end, and I shall rewrite it." Such doings might seem unjustifiable to us; but then we have it in our minds that law reports are "authority," and that may be a prejudice which we ought to remove. Let us remember that until lately in the chambers, not only of conveyancers, but of special pleaders and equity draftsmen pupils were busily engaged in copying manuscript precedents. Access to your master's precedent books was no inconsiderable part of the return that you obtained for the fee that you paid him. In this way an enormous mass of manuscript must have been compiled. Now let us suppose an editor attempting to re-establish the true text of the bills and answers of that eminent equity draftsman Mr. A. B. or of the declarations and pleas of Mr. C. D. the famous special pleader, and having no better material than the precedent books compiled by the grandsons in law of these distinguished gentlemen, or, in other words, the pupils of their pupils. We do not envy such an editor his task. Pupils will at times be careless, drowsy, frivolous. But that is by no means all. They will alter the precedents that they copy to meet changes in the law or changes of fashion. What is more, they will sometimes be wiser than their masters, at all events in their own esteem. They will begin improving the transmitted text, and then belike they will discover that consistent improvement is a difficult or a tedious business and after a while will fall back on straightforward transcription. They will remember, or they think that they will remember, what they themselves have done, and, after all, these books of precedents are intended for no eyes but their own. Now we do not say that the analogy is perfect, still we imagine that the lawyer of Edward II.'s day regarded his copy of reported debates rather as we should regard a manuscript volume of precedents in pleading than as we regard our law reports. He studied it in order that he might be prepared to make the correct moves, "the book moves" we might call them, in the complicated game that he was learning to play; but he did not think that the Court would be bound to decide a given case in a given way because he had a similar case in his book. It was with no sense of responsibility to the public or to anybody but himself that he made his collection of cases, and he felt himself free not only to omit, to curtail, to condense, but also to polish, to augment, to explain and even to rewrite, if thereby he could make his precedents more instructive.

Lastly—for we must bring to an end these preliminary remarks—let us recall the fact that when we are dealing with the reports of a much later time, especially the seventeenth century, we have no scruple about saying that there were reporters and reporters, and that if some of them did their work admirably well, others did their work very badly. Strong words concerning certain reporters have fallen from the Bench before now, and until recently a well-read lawyer was expected to know that this or that volume was, to put it mildly, "not a book of high authority." We suppose that the veriest beginner might be heard to say in court that some case reported by Keble, or Siderfin, or Comberbach is worthless. But the further back we go from our own age, the more unwilling are we to make similar remarks about the reports that come to our hands. This is very natural. We feel that we can understand the law of Charles II.'s reign. We have a great mass of information about it, and we can realise its practical import. But who are we—this question must often arise in an editor's mind—who are we that we should be talking of the law of Edward II.'s reign with that sort of confidence which would justify us in condemning a report as obviously incorrect? Do we really understand the mechanism of those real actions so well that we can affirm that a certain case must be misreported? An editor is shy of saying anything of the kind. The proverb about the workman who complains of his tools is one that we repeat to ourselves in order that we may not hear it from others. And yet, if we make a rational estimate of probabilities, we shall be inclined to guess that the worst reports of the seventeenth century have their peers in some of those notes of cases which come to us from the hands of the medieval apprentices. Of apprentices some are idle. But perhaps we have dwelt too long among generalities.

XII

Statesmanship in an "&c."

An article by Maitland entitled "Elizabethan Gleanings" was published in the English Historical Review *in 1900. The first part of it, which he called "Defender of the Faith, and so forth," is reproduced below, except for his footnotes. He was misled by Sir Thomas Hardy's introduction to the Charter Rolls in believing that the use of "&c." in the formal title of an English sovereign was original with Elizabeth I. It was pointed out in 1910 by A. F. Pollard in his* History of England from the Accession of Edward VI to the Death of Elizabeth *(pp. 194-195) that Mary, Elizabeth's half-sister and immediate predecessor on the throne, had used it in her title in the early months of her reign. She did this to avoid styling herself Supreme Head of the Church of England, as Henry VIII and Edward VI had done, for Mary, a devoted papalist, believed that that supremacy was vested in the pope by divine law. After the suppression of a revolt strengthened her position she omitted the "&c.," and shortly there-*

after royal ecclesiastical supremacy was explicitly rejected by act of parliament. It appears, therefore, that the "happy thought" of what Maitland called "etceteration" at the beginning of Elizabeth's reign was not a novelty. The "stroke of genius" was a statesmanlike decision to follow a precedent that must have been very well known.

"Defender of the Faith, and so forth"

For nearly two hundred and fifty years the solemn style and title of the king or queen of this country ended with the words "and so forth," or in Latin *et caetera.* On the first day of the nineteenth century a change was made. Queen Victoria's grandfather became king of a "United Kingdom" of Great Britain and Ireland. He ceased to be king of France. He also ceased to be "and so forth."

Had this phrase always been meaningless? I venture to suggest that it had its origin in a happy thought, a stroke of genius.

If we look at the book to which we naturally turn when we would study the styles and titles of our English kings, if we look at Sir Thomas Hardy's introduction to the Charter Rolls, we shall observe that the first sovereign who bears an "&c." is Queen Elizabeth. Now let us for a moment place ourselves in the first days of her reign. Shall we not be eager to know what this new queen will call herself, for will not her style be a presage of her policy? No doubt she is by the Grace of God of England, France, and Ireland Queen. No doubt she is Defender of the Faith, though we cannot be sure what faith she will defend. But is that all? Is she or is she not Supreme Head upon earth of the Church of England and Ireland?

The full difficulty of the question which this young lady had to face so soon as she was safely queen may not be justly appreciated by our modern minds. We say, perhaps, that acts of parliament had bestowed a certain title, and had since been repealed by other acts of parliament. But to this bald statement we must make two additions. In the first place, one at least of the Henrician statutes had declared that the headship of the church was annexed to the kingship by a bond stronger and holier than any act of parliament: to wit, by the very word of God. In the second place, one of the Marian statutes had rushed to the opposite limit. It had in effect declared that Henry's ecclesiastical supremacy had all along been a nullity. It had indeed excused Queen Mary's temporary assumption of a title that was not rightfully hers, and documents in which the obnoxious phrase occurred were not for that reason to be invalid; but it applauded Mary for having seen the error of her ways, and having of her own motion rejected a title which no parliament could lawfully confer.

It was a difficult problem. On both sides there were men with extreme opinions, who, however, agreed in holding that the solution of the question was not to be found in any earthly statute book. That question had been answered for good and all in one sense or the other by the *ius divinum*, by the word of God. We know that Elizabeth was urged to treat the Marian statutes as void or voidable, because passed by a parliament whose being was unlawful, since it was summoned by a queen who had unlawfully abdicated her God-given headship of the church. This, if in our British and Calvinian way we make too free with the Greek version of Thomas Lüber's name, we may call the opinion of the immoderate Erastians:—what God has joined together man attempts to put asunder "under pain of nullity." At the opposite pole stood a more composite body, for those who would talk of the vanity of all attempts to rob Christ's vicar of his vicariate were being reinforced by strange allies from Geneva, where Calvin had spoken ill of Henricianism. Then between these extremes there was room for many shades of doctrine, and in particular for that which would preach the omnicompetence of parliament.

Then a happy thought occurs. Let her highness etceterate herself. This will leave her hands free, and then afterwards she can explain the etceteration as occasion shall require. Suppose that sooner or later she must submit to the pope, she can still say that she has done no wrong. She can plead that, at least in some of his documents, King Philip, the catholic king, etceterates himself. There are always, so it might be said, some odds and ends that might conveniently be packed up in "and so forth." What of the Channel Islands, for example? They are not parts of England, and they are hardly parts of France. Besides, even Paul IV would be insaner than we think him, if, when securing so grand a prize as England, he boggled over an &c. And then, on the other hand, if her grace finds it advisable, as perhaps it will be, to declare that the Marian statutes are null, she cannot be reproached with having been as bad as her sister, for we shall say that no reasonable man, considering all that has happened, can have doubted that the "&c." signified that portion of King Henry's title and King Edward's title which, for the sake of brevity, was not written in full. Lastly, suppose that the parliament which is now to be summoned is willing to go great lengths in an Erastian and protestant direction, no harm will have been done. Indeed, hereafter the queen's highness in her exercise of her ecclesiastical supremacy may find it advisable to assert that this supremacy was in being before any parliament recognized its existence, and therefore is not to be controlled even by the estates of the realm. Therefore let her be "defender of the faith, and so forth." He who knows what faith is "the" faith will be able to make a good guess touching the import of "and so forth."

And now it must be allowed that, though, so far as I am aware, Elizabeth if the first sovereign of this country who is solemnly etceterated, there may seem to be evidence to the contrary. It had been usual in certain classes of records to abbreviate the king's style. A king whose full style was Henry, by the Grace of God King of England, Lord of Ireland, Duke of Normandy and Aquitaine, and Count of Anjou, might well become upon a roll *H. d. g. Rex Angl. &c.* What I believe to be new in Elizabeth's reign is the addition of "&c." to an unabbreviated style. When she has called herself Queen of England, France, and Ireland, and Defender of the Faith, she has given herself all the titles that were borne by her father and brother, save one only, and in the place of that one she puts "&c." The change is the more remarkable because of all people who have ever reigned in England her immediate predecessors had the best excuse for an etceteration. But no: whatever King Philip's Spanish chancery may have done, King Philip and Queen Mary are not etceterated in solemn English documents. The whole wearisome story must be told: Jerusalem must not be forgotten, nor Tyrol. Even the town-clerk at Cambridge, when he is writing out the borough accounts, will write of Flanders and Milan. Then comes Elizabeth with her conveniently short title, with no duchies, archduchies, and counties to be enumerated; and yet she must be &c.

Now let us discover, if we can, the moment of time at which the etceteration began. So to do is the more important because I am not in a position to contend that this addition to the royal style is to be found in every place in which, if my theory be true, it ought to occur. In particular any one who relied only on the officially printed volumes of statutes might infer that the change took place before the parliament of 1563, but after the parliament of 1559. On the other hand, we may see the little syllable in a writ of 21 Jan. 1559 which prorogued parliament from the 23rd to the 25th of that month. Occasionally a clerk will make a slip, an omissive slip: especially, by leaving unmodified an old formula which he ought to modify. So let us look at the very first document in which Queen Elizabeth announced her royal will and pleasure. In Humfrey Dyson's collection at the British Museum lies the proclamation, "imprynted at London by Richard Jugge," which tells us how it hath pleased Almighty God to call to his mercy out of this mortal life, to our great grief, "our deerest suster of noble memory," and how the kingdoms of England, France, and Ireland, "with all maner titles and rights thereunto in any wise apperteyning," have come to Us, "Elizabeth, by the grace of God Queene of Englande Fraunce and Ireland defendour of the fayth. &c."

A little later Mary's body was borne to the grave, and there was heraldic display, of which an apparently official account is extant. Heralds are bound to be careful of titles. The late queen had a lengthy title, but it must be recited at full length. Then, when the dirge has been chanted and the crowd is questioning whether many more dirges will be chanted in England, comes the demand for a loyal shout for a new queen, whose title is brief, but who is something that her sister was not: for she is &c.

Then we know that parliament had hardly assembled (25 Jan.) before the commons appointed (30 Jan.) a committee to consider the validity of the summons which had called them together, and of the writs by virtue whereof some of Mary's last parliaments were holden. The committee reported (3 Feb.) that the omission of the words *Supremum Caput* was no cause of nullity. I should suppose that Elizabeth's ministers had by this time decided—and surely it was a wise decision—that whatever ecclesiastical changes were to be made should be made in a straightforward manner by repeal, and should not be attempted by means of a theory which Roman catholics and Calvinists would accuse of blasphemy and the plain man would charge with chicane. It may be, therefore, that they never had to rely on their "&c."; but some of us would gladly have been present at the deliberations of that committee.

Some years later certain English members of the Roman church were consulting some high authority —not the pope himself, but some high authority— touching the course of conduct that they ought to pursue towards a queen whom Pius V had denounced as excommunicate and deposed. Their questions and the answers that were given thereto were published by Dr. Creighton in this Review. These scrupulous persons desire to know whether

Elizabeth may be called Queen of England, and if so, whether the "&c." may be added. Question and answer run as follows:—

> Cum Elizabetha in forma titulorum adiungat in fine "et caetera," quo intelligitur esse ecclesiae supremum caput, quoniam eo excepto omnes alii tituli expresse nominantur, an catholici hoc intelligentes possunt salva fidei professione etiam illam particulam "et caetera" adiungere?
>
> Licet haeretici per illam vocem "et caetera" intelligant caput ecclesiae Anglicanae, non coguntur tamen catholici ita eam intelligere: ea enim vox indifferens est ad alia multa: immo vox est quae ut plurimum apponi solet in titulis aliorum regum.

> [Inasmuch as Elizabeth adds at the end of her titles the words "and so forth," which are understood to stand for *supreme head of the church,* since all her other titles are explicitly mentioned, can Catholics, knowing this, conscientiously add that phrase "and so forth"?
>
> Granted that heretics take that expression "and so forth" to mean *head of the church of England,* Catholics are not obliged to give it that meaning, because it is used in many other senses; it very often figures in the titles of other monarchs.]

If, then, we see significance in this "&c.," we are only seeing what was seen by some at least of Elizabeth's subjects, and the brain to which *illa particula* occurred seems to deserve credit for its ingenuity. Catholic and Calvinist can say that this is a *vox indifferens* common in regal styles. On the other hand the champions of a divinely instituted caesaro-papalism will observe that all Elizabeth's possible titles, except one, have been expressly named.

For all this we might fear that we were making much ado about nothing, and discovering deep policy in some clerk's flourish, were it not for a piece of evidence that remains to be mentioned. At the Record Office is preserved a paper on which Cecil has scribbled memoranda. It is ascribed to 18 Nov. 1558, the second day of Elizabeth's reign. Apparently the secretary is taking his mistress's pleasure about a great variety of matters, and, as he does so, he jots down notes which will aid his memory. Ambassadors must be sent to foreign princes; a new great seal must be engraved; a preacher must be selected to fill the pulpit at Paul's Cross next Sunday. Then, among these notes—which should be photographed, for no print could represent them—we find the following:—

> A commission to make out wryttes for y[e] parlement touchyng &c. in y[e] style of wryttes.

This seems to me proof positive that "&c. in the style of writs" was the outcome, not of chance but of deliberation—of a deliberation that took place at the first moment of the reign in the highest of high quarters.

So we might expand the symbol thus:—

&c. = and (if future events shall so decide, but not further or otherwise) of the Church of England and also of Ireland upon earth the Supreme Head.

www.ingramcontent.com/pod-product-compliance
Lightning Source LLC
Chambersburg PA
CBHW021647110726
47902CB00007B/1864
9780520315419